HANGING ON IN THERE

HANGING ON IN THERE

An Essay in Meaning

SELECTED POEMS *of* MARIE NOËL

Presented and translated by
PAULINE MATARASSO

With a Foreword by BISHOP ERIK VARDEN, O.C.S.O.

CLUNY
Providence, Rhode Island

CLUNY MEDIA EDITION, 2022

For more information regarding this title
or any other Cluny Media publication,
please write to info@clunymedia.com, or to
Cluny Media, P.O. Box 1664, Providence, RI 02901

VISIT US ONLINE AT WWW.CLUNYMEDIA.COM

ISBN: ###-##########

Cover design by Clarke & Clarke
Cover image: Vincent van Gogh, *View from Theo's Apartment*,
1887, oil on canvas
Courtesy of Wikimedia Commons

CONTENTS

This book is for two dear friends who have between them brought it into being: Erik Varden, O.C.S.O., bishop of Trondheim, and Eric Southworth, fellow of St. Peter's College, Oxford, who share a deep love and admiration for the writings of Marie Noël, both poetry and prose.

Fr. Erik invented the book before it had blown into my mind, sending off half a dozen random poems to Cluny Media, a publisher being an essential partner in the process. His belief in it has never wavered.

Eric Southworth has read and commented on the poems as they were hammered out on the anvil. Without his unfailing encouragement I shouldn't have had the self-belief to see the project through. Translating is one thing; translating poems is another.

I should like to give a special word of thanks to John Emmet Clarke of Cluny Media whose enthusiasm, when offered a handful of translated poems (the easiest) and an embryonic plan, has brought this book into being. To work in tandem with a publisher is every author's wish and I am equally grateful for his skills and thoughtfulness.

PREFACE

TRUTH, SENSE, MEANING: words which define themselves differently in different contexts, everyday words of which one at least reaches to the stars, words which overlap and can find themselves in contradiction, as in "truth makes no sense," these are words that cannot be avoided by critics and biographers. They will be in the background when they are not on the page, and I would not feel confident in undertaking to write about, let alone analyse, someone's life unless I was familiar with that person's language, indeed with their vernacular.

For Marie Noël truth was a property of God. St. John gives to Christ the claim: I am the Truth, rendering truth at once utterly remote and intimately present. Marie Noël worshipped a God whom she knew better than the back of her hand, yet not at all, and whose purposes rarely made sense. Looking up at him, on good days she saw the cloudy underside of truth, which is meaning.

From childhood on, her life did not make sense to her either: she was a child who did not fit in, who lived in a contradiction of terms. Finding that intolerable, she slipped sideways into music. Music and then poetry, which, instead of defining, opens windows onto vistas of meaning. In poetry words become fluid, symbol speaks to symbol and all is open-ended. Poetry offered her a medium in which she could learn to know herself, to work out her meaning, while hiding from an alien world. Meaning does not flourish in a context that makes sense.

Pauline Matarasso

FOREWORD

IN THE EARLY SUMMER OF 1935, the Petit Palais in Paris put on a splendid exhibition of Italian art from Cimabue to Tiepolo. In retrospect we consider it a fateful time. Hitler was preparing the Nuremberg Laws, to be implemented on September 15. A menacing front was building up in Europe. Yet still there was peace. The exhibition catalogue could acknowledge, seemingly without disingenuousness, "the infinitely generous gesture of Monsieur Mussolini" that had made the display possible.

Among the visitors was a 52-year-old lady from Auxerre whose spinsterish appearance, in its studied ordinariness, was a kind of armour strategically assumed to protect, as far as possible, a soul of exquisite sensibility, that is, a supremely vulnerable soul. Her name was Marie Rouget, her *nom de plume* Marie Noël. She could feel in her bones the storm brewing in Europe, though for a few precious hours she forgot all about it. "Such a dazzling thing," she wrote to a friend in an attempt to describe the exhibition. It had seemed to her, she went on, like a visual *Te Deum*. She was still in rather a daze when she stepped out of the Petit Palais and descended into the bowels of the Paris Metro. There she had this singular experience:

> On the North-South line, at the entrances to two tunnels going in opposite directions, the vaults bear these indications: on one side, "Montparnasse," on the other, "Montmartre." On the one hand, the Mount of Apollo and the muses, of pleasures, on the other, the Mount of Martyrs, of renouncement and crosses; on the one hand, paganism, on the other, Christianity. One finds oneself on the platform. One must choose. This left me for a moment very perplexed. I should have liked to be able to go in both directions at once.

This is a shrewd self-portrait. The drama interior to the subject is made intelligible, as in the art she had just admired, by the setting in which it is drawn.

The sense of being torn apart by conflicting yet constitutional necessities had once brought Marie Noël to the edge of breakdown. On the one hand, she yearned for God with an intensity that baffled her. It drew her to leave all created things behind to seek the Lord as he is in his ineffable glory: a call to holiness. On the other hand, her vocation to poetry drew her to plumb the depth of the human condition, to consider it not merely with curiosity but with a compassion that, of its nature, withholds judgment. Would she not have to choose one to the exclusion of the other? Could she be true to herself without putting a part of herself to death?

In the throes of this dilemma, devoured by scruples, she had written, in 1918, her first letter to a Parisian priest who would guide her, until he died in 1944, towards freedom and wholeness. He enabled her to discover the range of Christ's grace whose hallmark it is, where our mind sees only implacable opposites, to make the two one. This priest, l'abbé Arthur Mugnier, became a friend. It was to him she turned to describe that momentary paralysis on the underground platform, a particular manifestation of what remained a recurring malaise. The wise pastor responded by return of post on July 23, 1935, with customary conciseness and clarity:

> Montparnasse and Montmartre! Why create opposites when the possibility of synthesis exists? Water is fire's sister. St. Francis sang the praises of both: "My chaste Sister Water," then the hymn to the sun. Christ said: "I am Life, and have come to bring you life," and so forth. Remain who you are without a shadow of fear.

Marie Noël needed to hear such encouragement again and again. Her battle against fear was not won in a day; it was lifelong. But she kept fighting it, determined not to leave unacknowledged, unsaid, unexposed anything she found to be real and true. Her poetry testifies gloriously to this endeavor. Rarely has literature been at the same time so embodied and so sublime. One thinks of that essential line from the Letter to the Ephesians: "anything exposed to the light becomes light."

To translate Marie Noël is a formidable proposition. It presupposes not just the gift and austere discipline of poetry, but a fearlessness like that, arduously conquered, of the poet in the face of both despair and the shimmering of uncreated Fire. Perhaps only Pauline Matarasso could have done it. Anyone who reads her introduction will be struck by what struck me: it reads like the account of one who, throughout a lifetime, has lived alongside the person whose life she tells, the account of a sister or a trusted best friend. That impression of connaturality is confirmed by the poems, which remain in her English versions resplendent in their integrity. In this anthology, we hear the true voice of Marie Noël bound recklessly at once for Monmartre and Montparnasse, only to discover that, beyond what she thought was the terminus of each, the two lines meet.

Bishop Erik Varden, O.C.S.O.

AN EVENTLESS LIFE

AN EVENTLESS LIFE tossed and shaken by inner weather like a tree; Marie Noël is known to us through her poems, some stories in prose, her Journal, and a selection of letters from a large and still unedited correspondence. She had no status, no profession, no money to speak of, no husband, lovers, or children: all attempts to define her start from these writings. Having little else to go on, we seek the person in and through her words, and believing we have found her there, we turn back to the works in the light of our own interpretation.

It is true that she lived at a certain period, within dates which can also be seen as defining her, but this is another unsure path to tread, not least with long-lived subjects. Marie Noël died in 1967. To the old among us that is quite recent. In 1968 the students were "taking over" the Sorbonne. The second Vatican Council was in session. She doesn't seem far removed at all, a great-aunt perhaps? In reality in 1900 she was already seventeen, and 1883, the year of her birth, sounds to most of us like another world.

France was twice invaded in her lifetime, and each time the horror was recorded by her in powerful poems. In 1940 German armour rumbled for three days past her house; small and indomitable, she crossed the street to buy bread by waving it down. Not an eventless life then, if one includes events that affected populations and over which the individual has no control.

As it happened, Marie Noël, or Marie Rouget, as she was by birth and baptism, had little more agency over the course of her personal life, which was largely determined by family circumstance and what were then the norms of provincial life, most of which have been swept away. She was born in Auxerre in Burgundy, a once Roman town, which rises steeply from the river Yonne to the magnificent hilltop cathedral in the shadow of which she spent her life. The family had long roots in and around the town, mainly as builders of houses and boats; its members, by the time she joined it, were an established part of the local bourgeoisie. Her father, exceptionally, had been sent to Paris as a boy to complete his education, returning to teach philosophy and history of art, the first, appropriately, at the boys' lycée, the second at the girls'. He married a first cousin, Emélie Barat, who had one saint already among her immediate forebears.[1] Marie Mélanie, born on February 27th, 1883, was their eldest child, to be followed by three brothers, Henri, Pierre and Eugène. The family network in the town was thus particularly close, giving the children what could be seen as security or felt as suffocation. For the child who would later emerge as Marie Noël, it was to prove mainly the second. Interestingly, Louis Rouget asked, not a family member or neighbour, but a close friend of his student days to stand godfather to his infant daughter. It proved a prophetic choice. Raphaël Périé was, by the time his goddaughter grew up, an Inspector of Schools, a man of wide culture and advanced opinions. He would be the first person she showed her poems to; for a number of years he

1. Madeleine Sophie Barat (1789–1865), foundress of the Society of the Sacred Heart, canonised in 1925.

served her as mentor, and he and his wife became a regular port of call for advice and comfort.

The family house was only a step from the cathedral, which would become her lifelong sanctuary. Its great tower looked kindly down on her when she played in the back garden, and in due course she learnt from its interior the mathematics of space and the narrative of time seen from the divine perspective. Hers was a cultured home. The father, agnostic and intellectual but also gifted at doing and making, was passionate about philosophy and art, a stoïc by conviction and, according to his daughter, "frighteningly lucid": no deviation from facts was tolerated. The mother was a Sunday Catholic, outgoing and welcoming, a great teller of stories (fiction was permitted to adults); mother and children were all musical, both Marie and her brother Pierre were good pianists. Next door lived the paternal grandparents. Grandmother Rouget was a fount of wisdom, good sense and traditional songs; to her little granddaughter she was also a comfort-giver. Marie was deemed "too delicate" to go to school (she eventually went to the lycée aged sixteen). It is hard to tell what physical condition, if any, determined this. What is certain is that the child was highly sensitive, and inhabited that narrow borderland of childhood which lies between anxiety and terror. Living for ten years in a house known as La Maison du Diable may not have helped: "there is somebody creepy in 'little cubby-holes,' in ill-lit rooms, in cupboards where dresses hang like dead people."[2] Stories of course were full of ogres, demons, wolves, and outside, in the dark, narrow streets, there lurked Men... She played a lot with her many dolls, teaching them their lessons, and, when possible, kept out of the way of visiting grown-ups (grown-ups in general were an alien species). But as she is her own best story-teller, I will let her bring

2. Marie Noël, *Petit-Jour*, first published by Stock in 1951, is the immediate source for her childhood experience, unless otherwise specified.

back to life the child she then was and to whom she remained true until her dying day.

> I remember when I was ten or eleven being struck with terror by the dreadful injustice of the fate of Judas...Judas forced into betrayal in order to fulfil the Scriptures.... The family was sitting round the table at lunch when these words from the Gospel flashed through my brain like dark lightning. I pushed my plate away. I can still see what was on it: hake in caper sauce. And I really liked it! But I couldn't eat another thing that day. Instead I ran off to my grandmother—my childhood's theologian—with my difficulty bursting within me: Judas forced into evil, Judas necessary, God unjust... it was killing me.
>
> But grandmother was quite untroubled: "Just leave it be. It's not our business, that, it's God's. He sorts those things out."
>
> Oh, what a good, light-filled grandmother I had; and when I was little how I needed her to pull me out each time I tumbled head first into an abyss.[3]

There were holidays too, spent some miles south of Auxerre, in the Morvan, that sparsely inhabited, thickly forested hill country, with its springs and streams. It was there that she fell in love with the wild wood, which would come to haunt her poetry, a place of beauty and peril where she once nearly lost her soul while rashly looking for it. But that was a grown-up adventure. As she looked towards adolescence, the landscape made a perfect backdrop for the Virgin Mary and accompanying angels. In childhood she walked hand in hand with the Virgin and never lost this familiarity.

3. Marie Noël, *Notes Intimes* [*N. I.*], (Stock, 1955), 57.

BACK IN AUXERRE, she started accompanying Grand'mère Rouget to Vespers in the cathedral. The time was drawing near for making her First Communion: she had been having daily instruction for three years from a catechist engaged by Mme Rouget for that purpose, but the pressure was now increased. The Jansenist rigour, of her mother in particular, became so negative that the child was overwhelmed—the word "sacrilege" waved over her proved too much. Bravely she walked out alone one day to find Mlle Ernestine and told her that she did not wish to go ahead. The pressure was promptly eased, her sins and misdemeanours ceased to be mentioned, although she was still required to kneel on one occasion and ask pardon for them before each parent and grandparent. The day of her communion was all joy, but to preserve the love of Jesus, an early death seemed to the eleven-year-old the surest path, so she set about praying for that. Excessive gestures are part of childhood, her earlier stand, though, had been rooted in the real: it had taken not only courage and determination, it was sensible as it avoided a scene with her mother.

Four years later she would make another request to God, also excessive, yet in a different category: she asked for three things, of which the first was less a gift than a commitment. It was, though she did not yet know it, a self-giving, and the reverse of childish. This time she was heard:

> When I was fifteen, I often prayed at night. I would kneel down, and, sometimes, God would speak to me.
>
> One night when I found him ready to grant me everything, I asked him there and then for three things:
>
> To suffer a lot,
> To be a poet,
> To be holy,

> Because at that moment it seemed to me that there couldn't be anything greater.
>
> To suffer a lot. He gave me that. I didn't know what it was! He gave it to me. I just had to say "yes." I have said "yes." Always.
>
> To be a poet. He gave me that. I wasted half…in time given to good works for family, household, neighbours, umpteen duties which crowded out the one that was properly mine.
>
> To be holy. God gave it. I lost it.
>
> I didn't give up all for him, ardently, madly, as I could have, ardent and mad as I was.[4]

The Church is now considering whether she was right to think that she forfeited the third gift. What is undeniable is that she became a poet, and the poet of suffering, and that she collaborated fully in these processes:

> When I was eighteen, I sold my wit to God as others sell their soul to the devil. In those days I was gawky, plain, sickly, ashamed of myself like the "ugly duckling," but I was witty… with a wit that was clear, quick and trenchant, and merciless as to whom it stung or bit.

The eighteen-year-old got a lot of laughter and some sense of success, but it also brought her sharp criticism from the family. So, having taken a good look at herself and decided it wasn't Christian behaviour, she went off one morning to the Lady Chapel and had it out with God. How could she sacrifice her only social talent? God waited with an air of reproach. But instead of a gift she offered a bargain: she would give up her wit, and He could pay His due when and how He wanted. She found it really hard at first, but habit helped,

4. *N. I.* 221.

> until over time I turned into the sweet little old spinster, unseen and unnoticed, to whom no-one paid attention whether at home or about town—no more than might be given to a dead matchstick.

Literary success would come, unlooked for, to the poet. But where was God's side of the bargain? Love? Happiness? No sign of either.

> I think actually that it was a gift of new sight: the ability to see straight away, not the ridiculous in people, but their flower, their honey, even in those who have none. So that now I love them so, even the ridiculous, the silly and the mediocre, that I can trot out my mischief playfully, just to amuse myself without hurting a soul.[5]

She had not waited for God to turn her into a poet. An apprenticeship of the practical sort was served from early childhood. The musical child of a musical family, song was a part of her life from babyhood. Little children were sung to sleep by mothers and nurses, and this child would one day write lullabies for others. Outdoor play was full of the songs and movements of traditional games. For several years she sang with her favourite cousin Julien, who lodged with the family while studying at the lycée. Her faith came to her down the same well-worn paths. The truths of her religion were first *heard*, and went on being heard all her life. She learned by listening—to her grandmother, her mother, the parish catechists—but above all, from the time of her First Communion she listened daily to the liturgy sung and spoken, mostly in a language forever strange yet deeply loved, a language that had its own music. When, a little later, she began to write, a tune would

5. *N. I.* 83–84

come first, then words to fit it, and often both would be written down, lessons in harmony being part of her education (she later both composed and conducted for the cathedral choir). When the words finally took precedence, rhythm remained an integral part of her poetic gift, and in her forties she boldly upset the classical balance of the alexandrine, "distressing" it until it voiced the disquietude of her inner self.

This over-sensitive child, desperate for love and frequently scolded and rebuffed, during her teenage years retreated within herself and became self-protective and prickly—what she terms "sauvage," a mixture of the shy and the untamed. At eighteen she saw herself as unattractive, awkward and ill-dressed. Exaggerated? Perhaps, but either way, little sympathy or understanding were forthcoming. This was the reverse of the daughter her mother wanted: a pretty girl with social graces, who would make a good marriage. Her admired father, lucid, cool and distant, was convinced that a little willpower went a long way (a lot was even better). She ends up being a problem to be sorted out, preferably by a change in her behaviour. It is perhaps not surprising that during these years, and beyond, she suffered with various health issues that were almost certainly psychosomatic in origin.

ONE STORY of the evolving years between early adolescence and an immature adulthood is told by Marie Noël herself in her Journal. It is the story of a growing-up, of a girl listening to her heart telling her different things, of hopes cherished and snuffed out. She tells the tale again in countless poems, the same only different, and we learn in those what the journey cost her. But as a poet she uses all the clothes in her dressing-up box, and turns her stories into the equivalent of parables, that they may be heard, but not understood... In the version in her *Notes Intimes* these variants are assembled in order, which imposes a logic, even if metaphorical. It is headed "Homes":

> I have lived in rooms in houses belonging to my father—the house I was born in and others—I have never had a house of my own. And all my life I have looked elsewhere for a house that was mine.
>
> As a child, this home was heaven, I invented holy adventures to take me there faster; in the evening I lay in bed waiting for a miraculous illness—a heart disease—to carry me off; I played ball-against-the-wall to find out from the ball the year, the month, the day of the week when I would be able to die and join God.
>
> And as I was very clumsy, the ball fell to the ground and I died in the flower of my youth.
>
> When I was an adolescent it was some wondrous chapel I don't know where, all lit up and ardent with prayers and incense. And there, veiled in white and candle in hand, in a passionate encounter in a darkness filled with angels, I met and was wedded to the King of heaven.
>
> When I was about sixteen, there started to appear far, far away in the north, on a wild hilltop, a house in the snow. It was an evening house, its windows lit from within. I was alone in the living room, alone with the fire. Alone and beautiful—(it is the only place where that has ever happened to me). I was wearing a white and green dress. The room was decorated with holly branches. I had nothing to do...I was waiting...on Christmas Eve, suddenly, without knocking, someone entered.
>
> Then a little later, I came down to earth one day and invented the real house of a real woman. I knew it, I had almost set eyes on it. It wasn't big or grand and looked onto a poor street, but it had a small garden. I knew how the furniture was arranged in the rooms and I moved the pieces around. I

> knew where the workbasket stood with the stockings to be darned...I knew the plates with the blue leaf pattern I would set on the table...I knew which door would open a little later and who would come in, I knew just what I was going to cook for us to eat together and which corner of the bedroom I would get ready for the cradle.
>
> I waited. The years passed.[6]

The young woman who was, by this last stage, grown up, if still immature, had emerged from adolescence with a deep longing for reciprocal love, marriage and children. None of these were to be hers—she would never have a home of her own, and this lack remained as an unhealed wound in her heart, one she eventually learnt to cherish. It is my impression that the house on the northern mountainside was the imagined background to a mutual attraction never openly acknowledged, to a young man as timid and silent as herself, who had, also like her, unspecified artistic gifts. All that is known, and this is thanks to her friend and first biographer Raymond Escholier who may have had information from mother as well as daughter, is that Mme Rouget saw it coming, decided that the boy was not an acceptable suitor, and told him his visits were unwelcome. He left Auxerre on Christmas Day, 1904, presumably to seek his fortune, and never found it.[7] Years later, after her mother's death in 1943, Marie Noël gave narrative form to this still living experience in *Le Chemin d'Anna Bargeton*,[8] a long short story in which she paints a picture as perfectly composed and detailed as a Vermeer, set in a fictional frame. A poem of unknown date, entitled "Chant de la Muette," or "The Dumb Girl's Song,"[9] from the

6. *N. I.* 122–23.
7. Raymond Escholier, *La Neige qui brûle* (Paris: Arthème Fayard, 1957), 93–96
8. First published in *Contes* (Paris: Stock, 1944).
9. See below, 171 and 247.

collection she was putting together when she died, has also, I am sure, this memory at its heart.

If little is known about this event in Marie Noël's life, less than nothing is known of any other love affair, and this of a poet who said that her work had three themes: Love in the "Chansons," which were those closest to her heart, Pity in those "Chants" written for and about others, and Death in the remainder. Escholier felt that her poetic imagination was a sufficient resource for the love poems, but the poems themselves tell, I believe, another story. Personal experience is the source of all her work—she writes, often in detail, of people and places she knew. Again and again Journal and letters provide the background, the necessary "clues"—for while she detested and feared curiosity, she needed the truth about herself to take form, and poetry was her private confessional.

The subject of her love poems is almost invariably abandonment and betrayal. The young man who has walked off, often with a prettier girl, remains an unforgotten presence, a source of unspeakable pain; he turns into "l'ami," the friend, but always the one and only; in the last year of her long life, in the poem where she enters death's kingdom, he is remembered ...and forgiven.[10] I do not think you can write poems like this over sixty years without an underlying reality.[11] And Marie Noël surely confirmed this when writing, among a few precious pages gathered together and published after her death, the following:

> One day the man I loved confessed to me naïvely, talking of another girl: "Her, it's from the heart that I love her. With you, it's on another plane."

10. "The Greyhound," see below, 191 and 259.

11. Benoît Lobet, theologian and author of the excellent *Mon Dieu, je ne vous aime pas* (Paris: Stock, 1994), is also of this opinion, 145ff.

> Which plane? And where might it be? It can only be in the place which is not the heart, the place surrounding it, outside the heart, as outer darkness surrounds and is outside heaven.[12]

This was not the boy too timid to speak openly of love and sent off by her mother. It is surely the one for whom the simple home in Auxerre with its small garden was conjured up, the one for whom the table was laid in the evening, the future father whose child would lie in the cot, and of whom she wrote: "I knew who would come in." Her longing had run well ahead of his commitment. No doubt they had much in common, or she thought they had, and conversation about poetry can turn the head, or the heart, when one is a shy round peg in the square hole of home. He just happened to be looking for something more, or possibly less. The faithless lover is the only person of whom she sometimes writes with bitterness.

But the Christmas of 1904, which saw a lover banned and banished, had not yet done with Marie Rouget. It had been her favourite feast until then, the one most waited for. Twelve years earlier there had been a new baby born in the family, Eugène. Now, two days after Christmas, on the feast of St. John the Evangelist, the elder sister went early in the morning to his room. Years later she wrote to Raymond Escholier:

> Today is the anniversary of a terrible day. If I have been such a prey to melancholy, when my natural state was light-filled joy, it is perhaps because I suffered a shock, two shocks...of exceptional severity. It is certainly exceptional for a girl of twenty to find her brother lying dead in his bed just after Christmas.

---

12. Marie Noël, *Auxerre et Marie Noël, textes inédits* (Saint-Léger-Vauban: Zodiaque, 1992, 28.

> That happened on December 27th, 1904—forty-seven years ago... My mother screamed aloud for weeks...[13]

A few days later, her father, without thinking, sent her to fetch something from the darkened room. She was found there, upright and rigid, having suffered some kind of seizure. It was from this time on that she took the name Marie Noël as her nom de plume.

SHE HAD BEEN WRITING POEMS for an indeterminate time in the privacy of her room, the forerunners of her *Chansons.* She gave to the little collection the transparent title *Songs of Cendrillon* (Cinderella).

> In it I innocently misconstrued all the rules of prosody and even of syntax. However, thanks to a brother's indiscretion, the collection was noticed...whereupon my godfather, Raphael Périé, set about teaching me the art of poetry.
>
> My inspiration in those days took pleasure in wild leaps, and, beyond sentences and thoughts, in shudders in trackless places, in the fear that slinks around in words, like a wolf that one senses lurking behind the dusk... It was all still an incomprehensible muddle, mixed up with childhood, and full of odd ellipses and bad French. I was requested to make myself clear, which deflected somewhat my poetic career. Without correction it might have petered out in some distant dead-end, of the surrealist kind, and readerless. But I was a docile scholar, I applied myself: with the help of the dictionary I learned the proper use of language, and to prove to my teacher that I was as able as any

13. The death was natural, but stayed unexplained. Letter dated 27:12:51. Escholier, 98.

> to connect ideas and walk in time to a twelve syllable metre, I wrote *Les Heures* in a few months. Then I went back to my belovèd *Chansons*.[14]

The juvenilia referred to remain in the archive, which is doubtless their proper place. Her craft she learned from her godfather, the art was hers alone, and Raphaël Périé fully recognised its quality. He came on a visit to Auxerre, read all she had written and talked to her parents. He then invited her back to Blois, where on that and other occasions she spent enchanted days being indulged and petted by the childless couple. Coming back in 1909 from a country walk with some dog roses pulled from the hedge by Périé and wound round her hat, she caught sight of herself in the looking glass in the hall:

> Wonder of wonders! I was pretty!
>
> I let out a cry.
>
> "What's wrong with your mirror? It's suddenly making me look beautiful!"
>
> My godmother laughed—she was good at laughing—and my godfather hurried up to join in.[15]

She was twenty-five by then, what was her mother thinking of? Why was she ill-dressed, unconfident, convinced she was a frump?

> That girl in rags with no looks to commend her,
> Desperate to find a way out of a world
> Offering nothing that will feed or mend her.[16]

---

14. *N. I.* 156.
15. *N. I.* 227.
16. "The Face," see below, 101.

It is not unusual for a child to be born into a family where it does not easily fit, and Marie Rouget was clearly such a one. Oversensitive, "strong-willed" said her father, and "delicate" in undetermined ways. Gifted she may have been, but it took her godfather to notice it when she was twenty. This raises the question of relationships within the Rouget family. Reliable sources are thin on the ground, particularly those touching her mother. We learn most from Escholier, writing during Marie Noël's lifetime, and from the poet herself, from what she withholds and from written material, both coded and direct. Once, when the mother was tidying the linen cupboard, the little girl watching, when asked what she wanted, answered, "to be kissed." Her mother laughed, kissed her on both cheeks, said she was a good girl, and life carried on as before.[17] It was Mme Rouget who drove the rigid and punitive preparation for the child's First Communion, she too who dismissed the lover deemed unsuitable. There will have been constant, if unspoken, pressure on Marie to get married, and disappointment evinced at her unhelpful "attitudes" on social occasions. The delight her mother showed at her daughter's first literary success was unashamedly to do with social standing and the reaction of the neighbours (pleasures forgone because the girl insisted on secrecy).[18]

This was not a family at peace with itself. Henri, the elder brother, was "difficult." Pierre, the younger, a sensitive man and himself a poet, suffered from a form of epilepsy, and died during the Occupation, in the same year as his mother. He was close to his sister and supported her regularly in family disagreements on her subject.

An unmarried middle-class girl in the early twentieth century had no job, no money, no powers of decision, her clothes were made

17. The clarity of detail in which this and similar episodes are recalled in *Petit-Jour* is telling.

18. Escholier, 154.

at home by a visiting seamstress and under her mother's supervision, her social life was restricted to her parents' circle, and there was no way out except marriage, a state which brought a bunch of keys and authority within the household. A girl either internalised the rules, or there were breakages of one sort or another: occasionally elopement, in Marie Rouget's case withdrawal, illnesses. That plea to God for suffering—in a sense it had already been granted, and what she was asking for was a way of living with it, of investing it with meaning, and eventually, over a lifetime, of transmuting it into love. Some young women in her position found release and meaning in exchanging one form of restraint for a greater: and she did consider at sixteen following Thérèse de Lisieux into the cloister, but the desire for human love came to override that wish. In the event she lived in a cloister of her own, an unofficial anchorhold. There was, however, one acceptable occupation for young women of good family and that was works of charity. Marie Rouget was approached by the parish: there was a catechism class for children, would she go and help?

The room where the class was held, in a ramshackle building without heating or any amenity, became a place of fun as well as learning. The young catechist found a new use for her childhood round-games, and wrote and composed songs for her pupils to sing. A grimmer assignment was sitting with the dying. At a time when death took place at home, the poor who could not look after their old and dying, needing to go out to work themselves, became dependant on charity for this necessity. The effect on the young Marie was profound.

MORE SIGNIFICANT than what she did for the poor of Auxerre is what these experiences did for her, first of course the effect it had, at that age, on her mental well-being, but also where it led her spiritually. It was during these years, and there were many of them, that she came to identify herself with the poor. They became for her both the objects and the source of the growing tenderness which was a defining part of her being and can be traced throughout her poetry, starting consciously with the *Chants de la Merci*. But the initial and life-changing experience came in her twenties and thirties, working in the poor quarters of Auxerre, doing what is now seen as lying in the province of social care. What these sisters and brothers did for her, rather than she for them, I leave her to tell:

> Blessed be those who in their ill-lit rooms
> Elsewhere, poor nameless folk of a poor town,
> Needy folk without mastery or means,
> Who have but little bread and that paid dear.
> During my dreary years on the long road
> Where I went wandering, my heart mislaid,
> They sheltered in their pain the stubborn hurt
> Left over from my girlhood vain and void.
> And having lacked life's staple, they and I,
> We drank together from a common cup
> Of misery. In deathbed they brought me
> To birth and mothered me; small as I was,
> They in their turn, weak as they were, without
> Return, became my children out-of-hours,
> Turned into my Sunday daughters, were my
> Easter sisters and my brothers singing
> Every Christmas in the parish choir, and
> In joy and anguish we walked hand in hand,
> Their hearts in mine, and through tough years when theirs
> Was the one kiss flowering in the desert
> Of my soul. They warmed me at the firesides
> Of old women, they loved me, they, the simple

And the true, just as I was, no fame, no flower,
When nobody noticed me, they loved me,
They loved me! O my God, love them in turn![19]

The lines above, written in her autumn years, are a looking back in gratitude from a great distance, but they reflect a shift in experience which would come to permeate her life. She had suffered an unsatisfied craving for tenderness since childhood. I give the word its full weight as it is crucial, it defines her. This flowering of tenderness described here, a tenderness met with and returned, was quickly reflected in her poetry, in the form of a conscious choice to write about the needs of others. The "Songs," of which the subject was herself, seemed suddenly egotistical, and she responded to an inner prompting to turn outwards towards those suffering, like her, but in more extreme ways: the *Chants de la Merci* began to creep in among the "Chansons" and then to preponderate, and with them came for the first time the word "tendresse." Close reading of Mallarmé led her later to the view that frequently recurrent words in a poet's work revealed subconscious themes.[20] I think that her own use of *tendresse*/tenderness has a similar undertow. These are examples taken from translated poems, and I am sure there are more to find. I have noted four others in *Chants de la Merci*, but none earlier.

My tenderness that a flight of birds carries away	"Weeping Over the Multitude"
And the poor tenderness that lies	"Will and Testament"
Filling the dusk with tenderness	"The Face"
Freighted with tenderness	"The Guardian"
From shadow a tenderness	"The Spring"

19. From Benedicat Vos, "The Last Mass." See below, 168.
20. *N. I.* 308.

Mercy, source of tenderness	"The Last Mass"
Misery filled with tenderness	"I Do Not Know"
If I suffer...so tenderly	"Song of Divine Mercy"

The child who is a misfit, whose emotional needs go beyond those her parents can supply, has a hard path to tread, a path which is ever dividing to open up perilous choices. For Marie Noël approaching thirty these choices were proving successively unsafe and unsatisfying. Her future as a poet depended on continued mentoring, introductions, luck, and a degree of social self-confidence utterly lacking. The chosen road to love and marriage was going nowhere. Home was a prison from which there was no escape. There were also her increasingly debilitating bouts of illness: whatever the causes, the symptoms were often incapacitating. There was of course God, but God is never a safe option, nor was she sure that she still wanted Him, since his road seemed signposted only to Carmel.

These conundrums were aggravated by the pandemic of horror loosed on the world in 1914. In Auxerre the Marne was not far away and within weeks the German army was on its banks; 80,000 French were lost in the ensuing victory, which saved Paris, and ultimately France after a further four years of reciprocal decimation. Marie Noël wrote four poems commemorating the deaths and suffering of that time. Two were published in 1930 in the *Chants de la Merci,* the other two held back until the *Chants d'Arrière-Saison*, appearing only in 1961. In "Prière d'août, 1914," she attains a new and rare resonance, reminiscent of Péguy, killed during the first week of the French counter-attack on the Marne.

Sadly and unjustly, these poems cost her the support of Raphaël Périé, that passionate internationalist and disciple of Romain Rolland, who found her patriotism deeply distasteful and came to the conclusion that she had lost her way and her poetic inspiration.[21]

To know that he no longer believed in her undermined still further her own self-belief, but perhaps worse was the perceived loss of his affection at a time when she most needed it. Yet the connection, however damaged, was maintained by her perseverance, and she always referred to him with unstinted magnanimity.

During the war her work with the poor was extended to the wounded, and by 1918 she was physically and emotionally drained—her hair in her thirties turned prematurely white. Her relationship with God, at the core of her being, was under strain as well, fed by and anchored as it was in her inner contradictions, which had become intolerable. Her own troubled words have become book titles: *My God, I Do Not Like You* today rubs shoulders on the shelf with *I Often Get Upset With God.* She was now thirty-five, and it was in the hope of answers to this and other questions that she wrote on her birthday to Abbé Mugnier, known as "le confesseur du Tout-Paris," who became a beneficent presence in her life for the next twenty-five years.[22] Initially the exchange remained formal, if kindly, on his part, complicated and stilted on hers, and might have stayed this way without the major breakdown of her physical and mental health which had been looming for some years. In 1920 she was ill enough to be sent off to a well-known psychiatric clinic outside Paris under the direction of a Dr. Page. In her luggage she had the manuscript of *Les Chansons et Les Heures,* which the doctor asked to see, after finding her unhelpfully taciturn. It took a lot to winkle it out of her, but it proved a turning point: after admitting that he hated reading poetry, but had spent the whole night reading this, he exclaimed; "Mais vous êtes tendre!" Given the password to her confidence, she opened

21. Escholier writes with sensitivity and eloquence about these poems and the behaviour of Périé, which she glossed over with typical generosity, avoiding a definitive break (177–188).

22. Their correspondence, edited by Xavier Galmiche, can be found in *J'ai bien souvent de la peine avec Dieu* (Paris: Éditions du Cerf, 2017).

up like a flower and gave him in return all her trust. He did not let her down. With his authorisation she went to mass daily at Bellevue, receiving communion without fail, often on behalf of other patients who asked her, and as the representative of "those who suffered most." According to Page, she was indeed that one, so all were held together in unity.

Within weeks he had sent her to Paris—on her own—to take her manuscript to a publisher he knew. That test of her mettle passed, she left Bellevue after four months to start the slow climb to a tolerable level of stability.[23] She slithered back down a few times, but never again into the pit where even God had turned into a hideous unlikeness of Himself. Where she had been, she could count on nothing: not on family, not on friends, not on her mind or her heart, and not, it now appeared, on God. The worst episode took place in 1920, probably just before her time at Bellevue, and lasted for what she called "the seven weeks of hell." She left accounts of the experience in both poetry and prose.[24] I find the poetry the more powerful of the two, for poetry, speaking to and out of the subconscious, goes where prose cannot. In five poems which form an extraordinary ensemble, "Destiny," "Ill-Met," "Song of the Guardian," "Storm" and "Dawn," she shares with readers, present and to come, the downward plummet and the slow climb back. These poems are the hinge between before and after: before had to die so that after could be born.

In order to escape from the stagnant and bottomless pond that her soul had shown itself to be, she had, in the poem and no doubt in life too, to walk across it on an uncertain bridge made from pieces of dead wood salvaged from Christ's Cross. What she had seen in the pond stayed with her, including the reverse-faced God

23. Details of her time at Bellevue are given by Escholier, 189–200, and clearly come from Marie Noël herself. He concludes, doubtless correctly, that her real need was for spiritual healing, and that she found this subsequently through Abbé Mugnier.

24. For the most complete account see *N. I.* 103–106.

of nightmare, somehow akin to evil and death—God at odds with Himself. Her spiritual life lay broken at her feet. How was she to put it together again? By saying Yes, said the Angel, who had been watching over her, and, indeed, she had always said Yes.

She went on saying Yes. And, as physical strength and energy returned, she reached out to embrace the big subjects. The first part of the Songs of Mercy predates the crisis. She was feeling her way then, writing about the hard lives of the poor that she was seeing daily. The second half contains the major theological poems, "Chant de la Divine Merci," "Appel au Berger," "Adam et Ève," which were written from 1922 onward. Both parts were published as one volume in 1930. It was a bold undertaking, achieved against the background of the dialogue with Abbé Mugnier and his necessary support.

The "Song of Divine Mercy" remained one of her two favourite poems, and one can see why: she has resolved the conflict at the heart of the Trinity—what she called "the combat of God with God"—by handing the initiative to the Son. She was at the halfway point of her life by then, she would still have time to move on from conflict, stretching out her arms instead to embrace the paradox of the Cross.

Her original approach to Mugnier had been ostensibly for advice on her reading, which had until then been severely restricted by the fact that a large proportion of French literature was on the Index. Even her father, the sceptic, had doubts about what she should read: she was a girl, after all. There is a lot in language: the expression *vieille fille* for unmarried women over the age of thirty speaks volumes. At thirty-five she was neither old nor a girl, and yet was living at home, strictly limited in what she might read, say or do. In this infantilisation the Church had colluded, had indeed taken the initiative. The Church in the person of Mugnier would now step in to liberate her, but first she had had to hit rock-bottom. The Abbé wanted her free: her true vocation was as a poet, not a parish worker; she was Mary, not Martha. He set about untying her scruples, the knots of her Jansenist upbringing. Like his scientific counterpart Dr. Page, God's psychiatrist was quick to see her childlike need to love and be loved: here too she must grow up. Through the combination of her breakdown and his gentle tuition, she did, while the suffering she had asked for at fifteen continued to be granted, but was integrated over time and transmuted into tenderness.

There were still events that would take place within the confines of this seemingly eventless life, and others, external, that would impinge, sometimes dramatically. The first combined the public and the private: *Les Chansons et les Heures* had appeared in December 1920. Hailed at once by the Abbé and noticed in a few journals, it was nearly a year later that an uncut copy, picked up by chance off a table, got passed round a small group in the literary and political world. There followed admiration, articles, publicity. A new poet was launched. The Abbé was delighted by this well-deserved success and encouraged her to enjoy it. He also encouraged his friend who would become one day her biographer, Raymond Escholier, to go to Auxerre on a cold spring day in 1922 and visit her in the family home. This was the start of one of her longest and most valued friendships.

March 1923 saw the unexpected death of her father. She owed him much: he had taught her to think, and had it not been for Grand'mère Rouget, she might well have followed him down Sceptics' Avenue, instead of merely getting mired in doubt. In fact his stoicism just wasn't enough, it didn't speak to her passionate nature, nor satisfy her craving for love, nor did it bridge the yawning abyss. But she could understand courage and perseverance, which together made up that traditional virtue, fortitude. Moreover, she had far more of it than he gave her credit for, and understood the nexus between courage and love.

> Courage...always...a lot...too much...dare I think that I might not have had such need to exercise all this courage later, if

> someone had opened up and kept for me, from childhood on, the sanctuary of merciful tenderness that I so longed for as the passionately loving child I was, and still am today.[25]

On his side Louis Rouget was the epitome of what in England would have been called a Victorian father; "absolutely not a man of feeling" was how his daughter put it, adding: "I don't think I ever heard from him a tender word."[26] They nonetheless enjoyed a close relationship on the plane of thought, and she missed him greatly. His death meant that her mother leaned on her with all her weight for emotional support, while burdening her also with a range of matters practical.

But she was able to cope now with whatever life asked of her. The crisis she had suffered, and still more the courage that recovery demanded of her, opened her eyes to her own immaturity. With honesty she acknowledged and addressed it. In the aftermath of her father's death she found herself briefly looking after a young nephew. Supervising the homework of a reluctant child was stressful, but when he providentially developed measles she was in her element, coddling, spoiling, reading him stories, all her maternal instincts briefly fulfilled. She told her friend the Abbé about it, but without dwelling on it unduly: Martha must get on with the serving.[27]

The father's death threatened to open up rifts in the family. Marie Noël was closer in temperament to her younger brother, Pierre, now married and father of the child with measles. The elder, Henri, nearing forty, was still living at home, but announced, three days after his father's death, that he was planning to marry.

25. Escholier, quoting from a note written for him by the poet, presumably while he was writing *La Neige qui brûle*, full of similar "inédits," 60.

26. Mugnier, *Correspondance*, 110.

27. Ibid., 119–10.

He was adamant that he wanted a civil wedding only. Panic! This was something her mother would never tolerate, wrote Marie Noël to the Abbé. How could she best help? The Abbé's advice and the sister's tact smoothed the path to compromise: vows would be exchanged in church, but there would be no nuptial mass. Marie Noël thought the couple well-suited, even though the union would involve a break with class, habits and traditions.[28] She was doubtless right; but death being no respecter of happiness, during a visit to Auxerre in 1930 they lost one of their three little girls to pneumonia—the second unexpected death of a child in that house.[29] Marie Noël was her godmother, and her grief—indeed her revolt—was the source of one of her finest works: the "Office for a Dead Child," wrung from her a few years later.

Despite old and new responsibilities pressing down on her at home, she allowed herself to be tempted to Paris on what became regular, if brief, visits, to publishers, to the Abbé, and to his friend l'Abbé Bremond, Academician and leading light of the literary scene, whose influence would lift her reputation to a new level. Between the two priests a competitive element came into play: Bremond was slightly piqued at having not discovered her, he, after all, was the literary historian. But Mugnier, the spiritual director, saw deeper. Bremond was drawn to what he called the *espièglerie angélique* [angelic mischievousness] of the *Chansons*, to their charm, but charm is always superficial to a degree. He also delighted in *Le Rosaire des Joies*—a collection she spoke of as a series of frescoes. He never plumbed the depths of the great poems of *Chants de la Merci*. It was Mugnier who came to accept, as he learned to know her better, that suffering formed an essential part of her vocation.[30]

28. Ibid., 108–109.

29. Ibid., 207.

30. Marie Noël's "Souvenirs sur l'Abbé Bremond' can be found at the end of *N. I.* 333ff.

This deeply religious poet was embraced by contemporary writers who were not themselves believers: Montherlant, Colette, Cocteau, Aragon among them. Admittedly they knew what she was talking about because these beliefs were familiar since childhood, they were a part of their culture, not yet seen as either ridiculous or alarmingly alien. But chiefly this was a land through which they could walk with her because she depicted it in the human terms and detail of a late mediaeval Book of Hours.

IN 1953 Marie Noël wrote to her friend and about-to-be biographer, Raymond Escholier: "My first three collections, although published successively, were all written at the same time, the result of the interweaving of three different inspirations."[31] In fact this is inexact, but Marie Noël had little use for chronology. She was always given to resurrecting poems found in drawers, pruning, polishing and slipping them into the next collection, with or without dates. At the same time, she disliked the idea of mixing what didn't match, and refused twice, once in 1921 and again in 1930 to combine the *Chansons* with the *Chants de la Merci.* The latter work, moreover, falls into two distinct parts. The last poem in Part I is dated 1919, the earliest 1907, while the poems in Part II, starting with the "Chant de la divine Merci," were written between 1926 and 1928, after her breakdown and the sojourn at Bellevue.[32] This is a notable gap and, more importantly, a turning point in her emotional and spiritual growth, and one can measure its significance in the poems written before and after—there is a quality difference. When she first engaged in parish work and wanted to use her poetic gift to complement the practical, she found that goodwill and empathy do not

31. Escholier, 277.

32. She makes this clear herself, correcting the letter to Escholier, in *N. I.* 157

suffice: "Ah!" she writes in one poem, "if only it were enough to have a tender heart." Lived experience must be added, and, above all, the finesse to extract the volatile essence that will fly with the lark. Of the poems in Part I, some take off and soar, others, the earlier, are hardworking, meritorious, but fail to fly. The poet had first to endure an emotional and spiritual penury and insecurity which would place her on a level with the poor she pitied: then she would learn to carry them up with her. She needed the "seven weeks of hell" and the months, even years it took to rebuild a scaffolding of health and, above all, a mature faith. The *Chants de la Merci*, Part II, ending with "Adam et Ève," are the triumphant vindication of what she went through. From a good poet she had become a great one.

When Escholier was working on *La Neige qui brûle*, and she wrote him the letter just quoted, she spelled out her three themes as: "Love, or what for me represents it, a passionate tenderness, Pity, Death." Indeed love, human and divine, was at the core of all she wrote, and while her personal poems reflect mostly loss and sometimes betrayal, those in traditional form cover a wide emotional sweep. Pity in her poems is like a product put in the washing, it enhances all the colours. There are poems bright with it, very few from which it is absent, and far from fading, it intensifies with age.

Death is in another category. I can think of no poet in whose work death is explored as often, and above all as closely, as it is in Marie Noël's. Death—and dying in its brutal reality, at a time when pain relief available to the poor came from the herbs grown in cottagers' gardens—forms the subject of at least one poem in each of her collections except the last. It haunts them all in metaphorical garb; it is also tried for fit in the divine jigsaw and no proper place is found for it. She saw death as the ultimate insult, the final cruelty, God's last word, his unacceptable comment on the waves of suffering that have engulfed humanity since time began. We had barely left Eden when the sound of our wailing began to keep the Son of God awake at night:

The God who made the earth
Nightly hears it weeping,
Hears his child say, "Father,
When's the time for sleeping?

If the groans of your creation
Do not quieten down a lot
I shall lack the courage
To be for ever God."[33]

Marie Noël's anger against God the Father is, in respect of death, intense and expressed without circumlocution. On good days she can find a counterweight in the figure of one man raised on a Cross high on a hill, and bared to the gale of grief and pain that sweeps across the world. But in the six sections making up the poem "Office for a Dead Child" the best its mourning mother can manage is a reluctant obedience to a deaf God, which she beds in some straight advice. Listen to your Son, she says:

Learn from him the agony
Of dying,
And the great pity and the crying
You should show to the misery
Here below.

In a number of poems she tackles the subject, like Grünewald or Goya, in all its physicality. In her last years she will tell a metaphorical tale, a tale of going out and walking towards an ending—an end which never quite comes, a final verse that leaves her poised, waiting... The language she uses is hardly ever that of theology, it is the language Auden admires in the painting, "The Fall of Icarus,"

33. "Song of Divine Mercy." See below, 59.

that of deep emotion set in, and set off, by the ordinariness of life. This is also the language of poets, and of Scripture. Theology is a man-made tool. God does without it; poets too. Mugnier sought to help her bridge the fissures in the Unity between the Persons, which tended to gape in her mind, while at the same time congratulating her on having a personality that was "not in the least theological, thank goodness."[34] He was confident that the Holy Spirit would smooth out her difficulties, if not in time, then in eternity.

DESPITE THE ABBÉ'S SUPPORT, in practical terms her life in the interwar period was not easy, but then, when was it? Her sudden success, noticed with surprise in Auxerre, generated unwelcome curiosity which she refused to satisfy, and which caused her to name, Linnaeus-like, a new hostile species to be kept at bay: the hunters, out stalking her privacy, her precious secret ever under threat, as they tramped the hills and woodland with their guns cocked.[35] The struggle between Martha and Mary knew no let-up, with Maman Rouget on one side and the Abbé on the other, conflicting duties lined up behind them. Mugnier of course knew better than to criticise the mother, but was unrelenting in his views on parish work [No] and her true vocation [Poetry]. After reading the *Notes Intimes* and her letters to the Abbé written in the thirties—"never a moment to myself"—it is hard to believe these years bore fruit in what many hold as her greatest collection, the *Chants et Psaumes d'Automne,* long in gestation and which rises to its highest point in the poem "Jugement," which took her five years to complete.

This major work consists in an examination of conscience, in which the poet speaks for both prosecution and defence in stanzas

34. Mugnier, 333.

35. "Song in the Wind." See below, 91.

which alternate between a well-drilled army of alexandrines at the disposal of the judge [God] and a jog-trot of octosyllables carrying a nervous but trusting child [herself]. Trustingly too, she went to Paris and read the whole work to the Abbé, by now blind. His comment, after listening to this confession was: "These verses need no justification. They carry within themselves their absolution."[36]

The *Chants et Psaumes d'Automne* in its entirety bears witness to a continuation of spiritual suffering, to an unfinished wrestling with God akin to Jacob's struggle with the angel. Not without good reason are the poems in the first half grouped under the subtitles "Chants Sauvages" and "Chants d'Inquiétude," nor does she lightly accuse herself in "Jugement"

> Of lingering too long in that vast solitude
> Where lie the sleeping monsters, weeping as they dream,
> And of drinking deep in the meres of disquiet
> Far more of suffering than was permitted me.[37]

As for the "Psalms," which include the "Office for a Dead Child" and her account of her earlier descent into the abyss, these are among the most agonised poems she ever wrote. Yet the fragile balance of mental and physical health was steadily maintained during the thirties and would never again be lost.

~

THE SECOND WAR of her lifetime found her in 1939 unsurprised—she had seen it coming. More clear-sighted than many of her contemporaries, she had never believed in Munich, and wept for shame when France left Czechoslovakia to its fate in 1938.

36. *N. I.* 213–14.

37. *Oeuvres* (Paris: Stock, 1977), 483.

Anti-Nazi in every fibre of her body, she proved herself in mind and will her father's daughter.[38] This was the second time she found herself living in an occupied country, and by 1940 it was one which had accepted its own defeat, a very different situation from that of 1914; but she too was very different, hardened like a mature tree which can stand the gale without its roots being loosened.

During the first months of the "phoney war," which many didn't yet quite believe in, Marie Noël was still finding moments of leisure. In a letter to the Abbé on December 30th, 1939, despite affirming that with a house full of unwanted guests she is reduced again to the role of Martha, she admits spending precious moments polishing and finishing "certain songs from my period of desperation which are melancholic and far from Christian. Their only virtue is that of singing (or, more accurately, weeping). But their pain now strikes me as pitifully small and dated."[39] I take it that these are the "Chants inquiets" written in the immediate aftermath of Bellevue. Fortunately, they were "tidied up" rather than suppressed, and duly appeared in the 1947 edition of *Chants d'automne* from which no-one of sense would wish them removed.

Six months later, on the afternoon of Saturday, June 15th, 1940, the German armour rolled into Auxerre, after bombing the town in the morning although it had been declared an open city—almost all the population had sensibly sought safety in the countryside, but there were nonetheless over two hundred killed, the Rouget house lost a chimney and had the windows blown in. Marie Noël, responsible for two immovable old ladies, left two accounts of this day, which complement each other while being utterly different. One is the poem in this selection,[40] the other a version of the same

38. Louis Rouget served in the Franco-Prussian war, was taken prisoner in the defence of Paris, escaped and got back to France.

39. Mugnier, 344.

40. "Out and About." See below, 157.

events given later in a letter and also included here.[41] Both reveal a woman fearless, energetic and capable of rising to any occasion. She was by then the virtual head of a household comprising her mother and aunt, both approaching ninety, the aunt bedridden and suffering from dementia. She was known and respected in the city and beyond. She counted friends and correspondents among the cultural elite of France. And above all she knew herself cherished and esteemed by these friends whom she trusted, and although this changed her not one whit, it freed her to be the person she was, who had been held captive for so long, in part by others and in part by herself.

Two days after the arrival of the Germans, Marie Noël was surprised to be summoned to the town hall as a "notability." There she found herself in the presence of the Préfet, the Deputy-maire and the German Officer-in-Command, all uniformed to the eyeballs. Pressed to take on a civic role, she eventually disengaged herself through a mixture of diplomacy, tart humour and a total refusal to be overawed.[42]

She walked home to her familiar duties, which now took the form of a long struggle for survival, primarily physical as conditions got worse, food supplies dwindled, and the occupying power hardened its grip to reveal an untrammelled brutality. Her much loved brother, Pierre, already fragile, died of malnutrition in July 1941. Madame Rouget had now lost two of her four children, and had spent nearly twenty years with her under-appreciated daughter as her support and carer. Before Christmas she had followed Pierre. Difficult relationships are often the hardest to survive, let alone recover from, and Marie Noël, in the centre of a family nexus, cannot have found this easy. The house, however, was not empty. Mother and aunt had been joined earlier by two nieces,

41. Escholier, 342–43. Further details can be found in Mugnier, 346–47, and below, 238.
42. Escholier, 343–49.

the daughters of her brother Henri, one still at school, one in her first job, who also needed catering for: more cooking, cleaning and hours spent queuing and seeking the wherewithal to keep bodies and souls together. The poet's weight went down to 37 kgs.

During these years, hardship defined her life. Never strong, she served what amounted to a sentence of hard labour. Extreme situations bring out the worst as well as the best in people, and pushers tend to get served first. Marie Noël would neither push, nor resort to the black market; however, country people would sometimes drop off vegetables or a few precious eggs, helping her to keep food of some kind on the table. The two old ladies had been difficult, but needed her; to the nieces she was a convenience with tiresome house rules—her kind of "mothering" was unwelcome (she tells the Abbé that she's now the cashier at the Guardian Angel Inn).[43] But harder by far than daily abrasiveness were the rifts which opened up in the wider family with the distribution of assets after their mother's death. Escholier, as biographer, maintains an eloquent silence. Marie Noël, in the course of a long letter to the Abbé writes of the pain of family disagreements: she has prayed all her life for peace and goodwill at home and God persists in turning his deafer ear. Her brother Henri arrives in April 1942 with his wife, and the house gets emptied of her mother's unfashionable but familiar furniture. The distribution of properties and liquid assets is unclear. Marie Noël, who has borne the day-to-day responsibilities, seems to end up with little apart from the family house, vast, as she says, and which brings in nothing and costs a lot in rates:

> I am poor now in every respect. I shall find it hard to make ends meet and, without a servant, to find the odd glade of free time where the wind of the Spirit might blow.[44]

43. Mugnier, 372.

44. Ibid., 371.

Moreover, there is no hope of her new poems being published or the old reprinted: paper is in short supply and the factory which had promised some has just been bombed.

> This, though, is happiness for me: to be on a par with the humblest women in the parish... Littleness is my element... the smaller I feel myself, the more stripped of belongings, of abilities, of wisdom, the less I have, the less I am, the less I weigh, the more easily I slip into the realm of Angels and Wings, and it's there that I feel more at ease than anywhere else.[45]

My impression of this family quarrel which caused her deep distress, after close reading of the only published sources (her letters to Mugnier and the *N. I.*), is that it must have involved relations outside her now very reduced family circle. Henri, who on his arrival in April '42 clearly took over the direction of their joint affairs, will have been in part responsible, but not solely, since whatever chill there may have been in the sibling relationship had vanished when in late '43, giving thanks for her daily blessings, she included among them "my brother, who shares his midday meal with me."[46] In 1943, a meal mattered. By then Henri had moved back to Auxerre for good, probably into one of the family-owned houses (possibly the one she had herself been making happy preparations to move into with her mother only a few months earlier[47]). It may well be that he was also learning to respect, even admire his sister. He will have heard from others of her courage, her qualities of leadership in a crisis, her reputation in the town. She had looked after his daughters, he would look after her.

---

45. Mugnier, 375.
46. *N. I.* 262.
47. Mugnier, 362.

Henri Rouget was not without courage of his own. Not fancying the prospect of getting trapped in the vast cellar below the parental house, when the bombing intensified during 1944 he dug himself a deep trench in the garden, where he would spend the air raids looking up at the danger overhead. Maybe he liked the thought of being *in situ* in the case of a direct hit. On July 30th, the Vigil of St. Germain d'Auxerre, Marie Noël hurried back from Vespers to the sound of the siren. As she sheltered in the cellar listening to the noise of approaching aircraft: a sudden change of rhythm signalled an imminent attack. Desperately she prayed to St. Germain: "You won't let them do that on your feast-day!" The engine-noise started up again... grew fainter ...

Henri rose slowly from his trench; "Well," he said, "they began their dive, we were for it, I got right down. And then...nothing! Off they went. It must have been the light."

The light was of the kind that ushers in a thunderstorm. Marie Noël put in a word for St. Germain, but in vain: it was the funny light...until a neighbour came and said he'd watched it all. The planes had come, and stopped, and turned, and flown away again. The sister went off to mass next morning carrying one of her last candles; her brother had knocked together a rough wooden candlestick to put it in: "Go on, you can offer it, it's all right!"[48]

In the only film we have of Marie Noël, shot eight years before her death, we see her coming out of the Cathedral after morning mass. Up a side road a figure comes to meet her, and they stand chatting, exchanging an affection that has been a long time growing. There had been hurts and resentments like brambles between them, but she had done her pruning, and as the plants sown in such places need cross pollination, he must have played his part.

48. *N. I.* 270–71.

UNSURPRISINGLY, and despite the Abbé's fervent wishes, she seems to have written little new poetry, although, given that the *Chants d'Arrière-Saison,* which appeared only in 1961, covers the period 1930–1960 and that very few of the poems are dated, it is hard to come to any firm conclusion. One extraordinary poem stands out: entitled "Message," it was written in 1940–1941, seemingly to de Gaulle, who was then in England talking to Churchill. In fact, she had never even heard of him, as she refused to read the papers—"full of lies"—and had no radio—"can't bear the noise." This strangely prophetic message is a plea to One unknown. It is confided to a seagull bidden to fly with it over the sea and appeal to the unknown saviour to come to the aid of France. It sobs in the minor key of Louis Aragon, powerfully, and yet, like him, without trace of sentimentality. With Germans billeted in the house, she gave the lines a medieval tweak to veil the meaning. She came later to regret cutting herself off from the news and thus from hope, and never forgot the thrill of hearing, in November 1942, the words "American troops have entered Algiers!"[49]

Brother, mother and a number of dear friends—this war was to leave her more bereft than the first. Very hard was the loss of the beloved Abbé who died on March 1st, 1944. His wisdom and affection had enabled her to grow into her God-given fullness. He could not know what gifts he was enabling, but he had the insight and the generosity of spirit both to hold the bird safe and encourage it to fly. Now he could let it go for good.

Two months later she would celebrate, all alone, in the solemnity of her heart, carrying the missal and wearing the white stockings she had worn on that day, the fiftieth anniversary of her First Communion. A few people asked why she was all dressed up, she

49. Escholier, 353.

kept her counsel. She was unable to invite those family members who had been present at the grand lunch on that day fifty years ago: most were dead, and those that weren't were not speaking to her. She spent the afternoon visiting her dead, they were more companionable than the living. She did though receive some flowers: she was not totally forgotten. And in the evening came the best present of all, the God-given one:

> A little path of peace, hardly cleared as yet, seems to have pushed aside, in making its way, the cruelties of the quarrel.[50]

FREEDOM IS NOT ALWAYS EASY, liberation never. Auxerre was bombed again in 1944, by both the British and the Americans. The first were preferred as being more accurate, practising *le vol en rase-mottes*, or hedge-hopping, whereas the American pilots loosed their bombs from a great height, resulting in what has since been sanitized with the expression collateral damage. At the time Marie Noël described it more poignantly as "discouraging the dead." Not wishing to be among them, she made frequent use of the cellar. It was not until August 24th, the day before the liberation of Paris, that the Germans, in disarray and with the Resistance at their heels, finally left Auxerre. Marie Noël was out celebrating with everyone else: "We Burgundians, we too sang and shouted in the streets for all we were worth..."

The singing and shouting gave way to the bumpy return to normal-but-different. Marie Noël was able to rejoice again in seeing friends, and, relieved of the straitjacket of family obligations, she found herself freer after the war to manage her own commitments. The Auxerre where she had been the plain girl, badly dressed and

50. *N. I.* 265–66.

devoid of social graces had passed away. Now she could grow into the role of local celebrity, the sweet old lady with the mischievous smile.

It is true that the role of literary personality never came easily to her. *Chants et psaumes d'automne* came out in 1947 and relaunched her, raising her reputation to new heights. People had only to take a train to Auxerre, ask the first person they met for directions, and get pointed to her house. Reluctantly she answered the door bell, fended them off when possible, too often felt sorry and let them in. They came from far away, they came from overseas, the grand and the simple, and when they couldn't come, they wrote, and when she could, she faithfully replied. This would go on until her dying day, in response to the works in verse and now in prose which also kept coming from her pen. These in turn were rewarded with prizes: six in the last twenty years of her life, many of which, I suspect, had to be received in person.

Those that weren't had to be paid for in other ways. In 1958 she was awarded the annual literary prize offered by the vintners of Meursault and the surrounding area of La Côte d'Or. The prize of 100 bottles of Meursault was presented at a grand dinner, followed by as many speeches as those present could rise to after their libations. Marie Noël found a new role for her brother Henri, furnishing him with an address not just gracious and witty, but dressed here and there in the local vernacular, learned in childhood visits to the family vineyard near Auxerre, where she would later do her stint during the grape harvest. She knew her wine, she knew what it cost in labour and she gave the best from her intellectual cellar in return.[51] Henri will have been proud of her.

There came one day that was like no other in the calendar, when she received from the hand of de Gaulle the Légion d'honneur. The prophetic poem she had written in 1940–1941 was passed fifteen

51. "Discours de la Paulée de Meursault," in *Le Cru d'Auxerre* (Paris: Stock, 1968), 13–19.

years later and without her knowledge to the General himself, who wrote a gracious letter to the poet. She of course replied in kind.[52] Then, in 1959, he came as President to Auxerre and presented her with the decoration for the body of her work. Later interviewed for television in her back garden, and still moved at the memory of the kindness in his face, she confessed to the world that he was "a real man, and you didn't often meet one of those."

IT WASN'T JUST the great and the good. Children too clustered round the old lady who seemed in some ways not much older than themselves: they sensed in her a real second childhood. They broke off their games and gathered round her when they saw her in the street. *Chants des Quatre-Temps* includes a nursery rhyme ["Comptine"] and a delightful "Child's Song," dated 1963. These may be set beside the photograph of her which precedes the title page and shows her seated on a hard chair, a baby in its baptismal glory draped across her lap, one of her hands securing it, the other holding a hand still tinier than her own. The baby's bigger brother stands at her knee. The two of them have their heads together, engrossed in the story one is telling the other. Neither will forget this moment.

Above all, the post-war years were a time of reconciliation, both with the past and with the future. The past in its entirety lay within the walls of the house—since 1942, her house. It held tightly embraced her childhood fears and tears, her girlish dreams of other houses to which she would escape to be another person, lead a different life, homes with their doors open to love, filled with the laughter of children. Instead, she had stayed there, captive, and served out a long sentence. Yet it was also the house in which she had learned all that she now knew, and had turned it

52. Escholier, 351–53.

into poetry. It had been faithful in its way, and in this extra time she made her peace with it, and in her early seventies offered her room this tribute:

> A poor little old room, dull throughout, no brightness or resonance...a little old room where all is faded, boringly patient, with its dozing stove finishing off a log in its sleep to the soft hum of its kettle...with the twelve hours on the clockface doing their twice-daily round...its books on the table, its untidy papers, its half-opened letters spilling scraps of news, scrapings of hearts—and, on the worn carpet, bits of thread here and there, fallen from the needle's eye...
>
> A poor little old room, nothing to speak of, but still kind in its assurance of rest, the sweet quiet it protects... until the day when, as night falls—they will have let the fire go out—the day when, about 5 o'clock in the evening, four strangers will come in and push back the table a little to set down a coffin.
>
> And when it has left, bearing away the inmate, then, losing body and soul, the poor little old room, in a daze, will cease to live.[53]

Her room in fact did and does live on in a way she never envisaged. Her furniture, her pictures on the walls, which meant so much to her,[54] her bed in its alcove, are very much as she left them and can be seen by many more friends than those who visited and wrote to her living. Even a room can have its afterlife, and the Cathedral continues to gaze down on her garden.

Death had to have its say first. The last enemy makes no terms with humankind. Marie Noël's furious debates with God about

53. *N. I.* 318–19.

54. She wrote a moving poem in 1963, "Adieu aux Images," bidding farewell and paying tribute to her "gens d'Images," whom with her failing sight she could no longer see.

death, particularly that of children, had been broken off unresolved. In *Chants d'arrière-saison* there are signs that the tone is shifting, the approach has become more metaphorical: she walks round and round the thought and looks at it from different angles and in various guises. The former anger has drained away. She takes up the conversation yet again in her final collection, *Chants des Quatre-Temps*, which she prepared in detail in the last months of her life, and in which almost half of the thirty-six poems bear a date of composition in the 1960s, several that of 1967. We have thus the privilege of following her to the very end. This last book, like her others, groups the contents by form and genre, closing with a clutch of twelve poems, often short, all cryptic and not easy to decipher, subtitled "Sentes pour le Dernier Âge" (Footpaths through the Last Years). They might be better summed up in the last line of one—"The Alleluia of the dust." Death here has lost its terror to become a meeting at an appointed hour, the hour when all hurts we have suffered are forgiven, and any unhealed wounds we bear become our "laissez passer" to the afterlife.

We know, as it happens, the circumstances of Marie Noël's death, thanks to Élise Autissier, who was with her at the end, one of two or three friends who were helping her prepare for Christmas, which held for her a unique place among feasts. She had spent all day sitting in her armchair, occupied with various things, but sufficiently unwell in the early evening for the doctor to be called. However, she made light of her symptoms and carried on until 2 a.m. dictating Christmas cards. Her companions then sent for the priest, and she sat for a long interval in silence until he came and anointed her, when she repeated all the responses and recited the Lord's Prayer, perfectly composed. She then received the sacrament and breathed her last breath on the instant...whereupon those present stood and sang the Magnificat.[55]

55. Autissier, *Auxerre et Marie Noël*, 236–38.

Prophecy can be in certain circumstances Janus-faced, as God was apt to appear to Marie-Noël. In the light of her death, there are passages in her Journal and her poems which will acquire for those who read them a prophetic dimension:

> I have fought so often for breath with the dying, died with the dead...that maybe I shall suffer less from my own undoing than I have in accompanying others through theirs.[56]

Paradox too can be Janus-faced, and ten years earlier Marie Noël had been much struck by a verse of Ecclesiasticus:

> Opposite evil stands good,
> opposite death, life;
> so too opposite the devout stands the sinner.
> Contemplate all the works of the Most High,
> you will find they go in pairs, by opposites.[57]

She had grown up in a period when theology had become detached from its roots in paradox, which explains in part why her trinity lost from time to time its unity: her sense of the Oneness of God was fractured by its own perceived contradictions: three in one does not make sense. Human minds subject to time's warp cannot stretch to the extremes of paradox which Christ was pointing us towards on the Cross: even for Him it took a resurrection body to incarnate them in open, yet healed, wounds. The poems which close Marie Noël's work are her legacy to us, her final commentary on the paradoxes in her life, soon to be resolved in a manner yet unknown to her, but which she and God together were preparing: the manner of her death.

56. *N. I.* 70.

57. Ecclus. 33:14–15; *N. I.* 315.

THE POEMS

THE ABYSS

A cross at the edge of the abyss.
It was here that a horror happened.
Pray!

It was here that a soul fell from heaven into hell.
It was here that she fought to the death on a dizzying slope with no passer-by.
It was here that the Enemy lay in wait, watching out for the moment of weakness, and as she gave way to it, seized on his prey.
It was here that the Beast chained within broke from its bonds and howled.
It was here that, directly she fell, all the sneaking griefs, those that had been mastered, collared, and seemingly sanctified, came running back as one to throttle her in the darkness.
It was here that no one came to her aid.
It was here that the angels abandoned her.
It was here that God turned aside.

Here, this horror happened.
Pray!

Les Chansons et les Heures

WHO AM I?

Work out who I am if you can, passer-by!
I am both what you think me and quite the reverse:
The unspeakable dust that you tread underfoot
And the nameless star that might guide you on high.

I both am and am not the way that I appear:
At once calm as a lake where the sky lies at rest,
So calm that in plumbing the depths of my eyes,
You will see your own image reflected there...

So calm, traveller, yet mercurial with it,
A will o' the wisp, a husk, a small dead leaf
Turning, dancing, blown this way and that through life
At the wind's vagaries—the fancy of a minute.—

A thing half wild, in its shy innocence enwrapped,
Which, like a swan pushing out from a river isle,
One day went gliding downstream through the reed-beds,
Slowly, avoiding the banks where the water lapped...

—And yet so gently brave, in spite of its alarm:
A confiding sparrow that lets itself be caught,

While its heart, that you feel beating through your fingers
Curving closely round it, will keep your whole hand warm.—

Strong as an army ranged at noonday, row on row,
Which fights and bleeds and dies, and yet never gives way;
That risks all, suffers all, triumphs over all,
Mute and yet towering—a wall against the foe...

Weak as a little child who ventures out alone
Feeling its uncertain way from hurt to hurt,
With sometimes such a pressing need of comfort
And, by nightfall, of a big hand to hold its own...

Ardent as the flight of the skylark, a bird
That from a dip in the ground rises quivering
At dawn, flying up in ecstasy, up to the sun
In fiery spurts, dare-devil—free, in a word...

More shivery than an orphan in winter's cold,
Hanging around stoves and desperately seeking
A source of warmth to huddle up to for as long
As may be, with eyes half shut and all else on hold...

Or again a young goat, so wayward and headstrong
That no one will succeed in getting her collared
And push home the bolt in the byre door behind her:
It will take death to capture and hold her for long...

Yet one who will give her whole self to the asker
In loving service to the love that disdains her,
At heart a beggar-maid timorous and faithful
With a dog's inclination to follow its master.

Get to know me...Oh do! But is what I've said, Me?
Now I've said it, it is false—And yet it was true!—
The tune my heart sings, is it happy, is it sad?
Know me if you can. But can you? Can *I*? We'll see...

Should my mother start to boast
To you, her guest, her neighbour,
Of my virtues loud and clear,
Shamelessly and non-stop;
When my old parish priest, who's
Losing it, starts whispering
What I confessed in the box...
Who I am will leave you foxed.

Oh, passer-by, had you seen all
My tears and heard my laughter,
When I had dared to bare my
Soul, and you had heard me out,
When you'd watched every gesture,
Followed every step I took,
Through the keyhole of my life
I would still be a stranger.

And when my soul aglow
Flits past your waiting soul
On Judgment Day, when heaven
And earth flame bright and when
God reads me like a poem
Line by line to the chosen,
You won't know even then
What I was here below.

But if you love me for one instant you will know!

SEWING SONG

The day he walked into my shuttered lodging
I was hemming a big sheet by the window,
Winter in my fingers, shoulders in shadow,
How long was it that I'd been there unliving?

And I was sewing, sewing, sewing...
—My heart, what was it you were doing?

He asked about our tools he'd like to borrow,
My feet leapt up and flew off to the parlour,
They seemed—so light, so merry was their ardour—
Like two little sparrows kissing the floor.

To and fro I hurried, scurried, hurried...
—My heart, what was it got you flurried?

He asked for butter and a bit of bread,
—On opening the box I stroked the wood—
New-pressed cider I then brought, and my hand
Caressed the bowls and the jug and the board.

Five, ten times I fondled these, and more...
—My heart, what were you looking for?

He asked me umpteen whys about things seen.
I talked about them all, the goats, the hens,
The weather and the people, while my voice
Caressed my lips while slipping out between.

So did I chatter, chatter, chatter...
—Tell me, my heart, what was your matter?

When he had gone, now noticing the hem
I'd left unfinished, I sat me down anew:
The needle sang again, the needle flew...
My fingers fondly stroked our unbleached linen.

And I was sewing, sewing, sewing...
My heart, what was it you were doing?

DIALOGUES

My heart is as heavy as the tomb on the dead
The tomb on the dead that is topped with a stone.
My eyes are forever in the back of my head,
What can I have lost along time's running road?

—Go and pray for sun so that my field may bear:
The ripening corn's your dowry.
—Yes, father dear.

Since the door was closed on his receding steps
The best tablecloth has lain still in its folds.
Has he quite forgotten me? How should I know?
Save that when I meet him, he says never a word.

—Do we live in a convent? That dress is austere,
Take it off. Wear the frilly one.
—Yes, mother dear.

I hurt...I don't know where this pain is taking me,
In my heart I hear a nightingale on fire
That is singing in despair, singing its soul out.
But I wait to weep, it's the night that I desire!

—Sister, the love song I liked better than another,
The one with the bird, sing it now...
—Yes, dear brother.

When will death come with its tread that chills the heart
That I may—at last!—find rest from my hurt!
Sweet will be the day when in the silent room
They will fasten the shutters to let me sleep on.

—Sister, it's time to go! You're surely not asleep?
The dance has begun. Quick, we'll be late!
—Yes, my sweet.

THE COMPANIONS

From my door I stood watching the Spring growing tall...
The tender sunshine fell at my feet, on my hands,
And my eyes dwelt on space, where paths reached for the sky
And fields on either side marched in bright livery.

In my heart was a place for the breeze and the birds.
"It's time, little soul, that you listened to our words,
You'll hear in the wind, in the earth beneath the road,
The steps of the belovèd coming from the wood.

"And if his light footsteps are singing a refrain
As they come skipping, follow him, he is for you,
Stronger than us by far! Just close your eyes and run,
And you will find in him brave worlds you never knew.

"But if all that you hear is the breath of today,
Here are we, fields, springing grass and the sky above,
And we will hold you tight, caught up in our dream...
No flying from us to anything less than love!"

Long was I left listening to the wind-borne voices,
My spouse was in no hurry, knew no songs to sing,
Used his slow steps to reckon what the crops might bring.
When he got here at last my door was shut and bolted.

By the time I opened it, it was late...too late.
A choir of rooks was cawing in a sky grey and bare.

I kept a wary eye on autumn drawing near...
Who will help me now to carry my heart's weight?

Where can I run to join again the girls in love
Who left me midway on the road and in the rain,
Where time dragged till it sped, and I moulder in vain?
Far away smoke spirals from hearths in happy homes

Resounding with the joy of voices raised in part
And unison. Snug within walls the feast is spread...
All their laughter and their calling has jarred my head
And the shouts of the children have fallen on my heart.

Oh! false friends who pet me as a grandmother might,
Spring, Breeze and Sunshine, what was it you were saying?
Your beguiling counsels have sent my wits straying,
And lost and alone now, you leave me to the night.

Then the wind said to me: "I am here! I am here!
And it's for you I sing, little soul, you alone,
This love song so sweet that no woman, not one,
Was so rocked and lulled by a voice in her ear."

"I'm here! I'm here!" repeated the Rain, "rat-a-tat,
My merry fingers are now tapping at your pane,
Long tales of mist and water are my true domain,
I go on and on, and on...do I bore you a lot?"

Then the Fog whispered: "In fleece too soft for feeling
You shall be shawled and nestled in my great white dream,
Sleep now, plants in winter do not feel the sap stream,
I will swathe the neighbours' windows for your healing.

Alas, companions all, please understand my pain.
Sleep? I have worked all day from morning until night,
My spindle has run out of wool, there is no light,
And my house should be full of work done or in train,

But of all that I've made there's nothing I can find.
The trees have all given their fruit, and the rabbits
Have reared three large broods with identical habits,
Even weeds sow the verges with seed of their kind.

The hen bird on her eggs will have fledglings to tend,
I alone resemble those scorched and trackless wastes
Where the barren sand whipped by each passing wind
Has brought forth nothing other than ghost clouds and ash.

Then the Sky said to me: "The clouds go on their way
Chilled, homeless and alone, without a goal in view,
And yet their falling tears quicken the seed below
And flush the cheeks of roses on Midsummer Day."

"Don't fret, Miss Nose-in-air," said Earth, there's nothing lost,
We've time enough to do our work, it's not too late.
Just let me have your heart, I'll wait for you, I'll wait!
And together we'll make good compost with my dust."

Les Chants de la Merci

PRELUDE AND EXERCISES II, 2

Loving is not the labour of a passing hour
Nor, sadly, is a tender heart enough.
Yours with its peevish bile needs pushing back
And down—far from your lips—and quietly settling.

Leave it, ignored, to welter in its sullen mood,
Use it to help another, weak like itself,
One fallen in a pit alone and lost at nightfall
With no way forward through a snarl of cares.

Give to that other way-worn heart the inner
Space you kept for yours—your own can do without you—
And bear it patiently within, day after day,
Wretched or foolish be it (even both at once).

Be you the one engulfed by the dark shadow
That torments it so: grumbles, grievances, regrets
And qualms, its idle chidings and its empty
Secrets (it may well be that this or that's a lie);

Lull it to sleep with chosen, soothing words,
Dismissing in the course of conversation

Its fantasies and fears, like flies which—as you know—
Will all come back and settle one by one;

Make yourself scarce when told, return unbidden,
Hurry forward to the rescue times uncounted,
Back-track as often to help it on its way,
And lose your own, complying with every whim;

Be present like a loaf left lying on the table
For each to break and leave and eat their fill,
Little, a lot, too much, without real appetite,
Just ordinary bread one can afford to waste;

Replenish from your store as your supplies run out;
As long as need still clamours, find one final gift,
And, if it it's not good enough and you get rebuked,
Apologise till that need, too, cease to exist.

SONG OF DIVINE MERCY

The God who made the earth
Nightly hears it weeping,
Hears his child say, "Father,
When's the time for sleeping?

If the groans of your creation
Do not quieten down a lot
I shall lack the courage
To be for ever God.

O Father, Wisdom deep and dark,
You are well aware
Why the world needs to suffer,
But the world has no idea.

Blindly it walks…and weeps…and I,
Blindfold in Joy abiding,
Know, alas, no more than they
Why humankind is crying,

Nor through what doubt and darkness
They daily plod. I'm heading
Off, I want to take the road
Those lonely feet are treading.

I wish, inclining my own head,
To seek even through Death—

—the very Death that you created—
That cry borne on mortal breath.

Death, that was first made by you
But never tasted, man below
Knows well and animals know too,
Yet it is unknown above.

Oh, take away the light from me
—the robe we wear and share—
If I'm to dress in human dust
I'll walk in the wind, bare.

My high degree at your right hand
Take from me, Father: I need first
To squeeze into a suit of flesh,
Prey to hunger and to thirst.

Wound me in my inmost being
So that in the warm blood's flowing
Through each vein, I hear the pain
That sears the soul in going.

Then spurn me like a thing accursed,
An outlaw on an evil way,
A son who took on human guise,
Left your side, and went astray.

A son brimful of wrath eternal
Who has taken flight
From the house of God his Father
To lose himself by night,

Lose himself in his great folly
With others likewise lost,
And while you watch, deaf to his
Pleading, die on a cross.

Turn from me, who now decamp
To join those down below: a poor
Man passing through, who drinks
From the wayside stream, a tramp.

I'll walk the roads alone and fast,
Like a man whom friends await,
All the hours until the last,
When darkness spreads its net.

The untamed horror humans suffer
Will come shrieking from my mouth
In the all-engulfing dark
When I have to swallow death.

Caught one evening through their sin,
Like them I will hear in turn
The tinnitus of the abyss
Vibrating in the bone.

That evening too, like these, O Father,
—heaven throughout undismayed—
That evening on my knees, O Father,
I, of You, shall be afraid!

Father, throw out of the door,
Into the fear around, above,

The son of man! I'll take with me
Only, of God's Son, the love.

God great and holy, without fault,
Since it is not your will
That by merely walking with them
I might free them from their ill.

And since pain is part and parcel
Of the God-given plan,
Just as wood must spit and crackle
To blaze up hot for man;

And as it helps your purpose
That the night of your creature
Should continue in some measure,
I will lend it a hand.

As long as you shall need, my God,
All the world's distress
At the heart of your mystery,
I'll bend to kiss its eyes.

But in your omnipotence
Impenetrable God,
What you need to do, do quickly,
So huge is it, so hard!

This throng is mine to carry:
The weight of heads bowed down
I will hold up in my bleeding
Hands, human as their own.

MARIE NOËL ~ *Hanging On In There*

The famished of this world
And the weak in their languor
Will seek from its four corners
My heart's bread for their hunger.

And as I lead them onward
To renew their lives in love,
They will feel their hearts lighten
Like the heavens above.

And while I keep them safe in me,
These lost whom I have found,
They'll see in lieu of misery
The light of heaven abound.

And seeing that I love them
And would die with willing heart
They'll think that you must love them too,
Despite their wretched lot;

That if they suffer, and I likewise
Suffer tenderly with them,
Then surely you in your abyss
Are doing what you can.

And so this suffering multitude
In my heart, their eyes tight shut,
Wait in hope on the uncertain
Good that may one day result.

The poor who have no knowledge,
Trusting in the starless sky,

Will mingle their own patience
With the work they cannot see.

Until the wonderwork your hand
In the darkness now performs
Is fully finished, I will hold
Your children in my arms,

The arms wide open of a man
Crucified, but while they
With sorrow crushed, and I with care,
Strain panting on our way,

Father, leave your doors flung open
So that I can bring back home
Those poor desolate souls, and those
Bodies chilled to the bone.

Have torches, tapers, candles burning,
Light the fire, let peace abide
Eternal. Thus, the last ache
Suffered and the last tear dried,

United, one and all, like brothers
Home after long years abroad,
They may rest from being human,
And we two from being God.

CALLING THE SHEPHERD

Shepherd, shepherd, isolated,
Lost in dreamland, look around,
All the happiness on earth
Lies beyond your cloistered ground.

Far and near the earth makes merry
Humbly clothed in commonplace,
Shepherd, where in this rejoicing
Have you made a dwelling-house?

Shepherd, where's the open road
To take you to some love, or other…?
Shepherd whose unlived-in hands
Are opened only to the weather.

Shepherd, drawn up by lowland air
To the skies fanned out above,
Shepherd, I am a queen who comes
To entreat you for your love.

Shepherd, where I walk, I weep,
A big kiss is what I need,
I am the Sorrow of the World,
Shepherd, will you marry me?

MARIE NOËL ~ *Hanging On In There*

In the wind and in the darkness
I've too large a flock to keep
On my own, in this foul weather,
None to help me watch my sheep.

The weary flock that I am leading
Through a land that has no end
Has been on such a gruelling trek
It's lost its way and cannot find

The sure path to its watering-place...
On the darkening sheep-walk now
A strange wind blows among the ewes,
Nudging them into jeopardy.

The wind from Nowhere takes control.
A false shepherd's come to steal
My lovely ewes: he turns them loose
To stray in a forsaken field.

Do you want me for your darling,
Shepherd? With my gypsy realm,
My flock of sheep without a fold,
My tears raining as we roam.

And in their benighted straying
Will you rescue them from utter
Ruin? Pour out your soul for me
To the last drop to make me better? ...

Come then!—but if you are seeking
To improve your lot, then stay

Away—for the dowry I will
Bring isn't even workaday:

The poor household of short commons—
A food-safe bare of wine and honey
Where each fast-day hides away
Its left-overs of hunger.

When your boots worn thin of sole
Grow scared to take the road again,
If you're lucky, some poor soul
Will pick them up to mend them.

Some old grey and grizzled crone,
Preparing for her own demise,
The sad affliction of your socks
Will, with a well-placed darn, disguise.

The flames will not burn high and hot
Between your close set fire-dogs.
You will have neither son nor wife
For company. The chill will bite...

Come then, my poor wretched shepherd,
Come to me and taste my feast!
I shall place God on the table
To break your morning fast.

I shall set close to your lips
God himself, in form of bread,
And your ewes, all crowding round,
Will then eat him from your hand.

To your lambs you'll give to drink
God, as you might your own wine,
And tiny droplets of his glory
On your hands will shine.

I am the Sorrow of the World
Who in the world can find no peace...
I am the vagabond that God
Comforts with a kiss.

He came from a far land to find
Me—poor and bare of foot was he—
Took me for his wife in wedlock.
I was lost. He came to me.

He tasted of the drink I'd mixed
Of vinegar and gall. With thorns
That pierced his brow he even
Took my sheep to the gate of heaven,

To the big gate bolted tight
To bar the fold. He led my flock,
A loneliness of sheep by night
In utter disarray and lack.

Down a strait defile he found
The pastureland closed off.
He has broken down the fence
With one blow of his Cross!

He has broken down the fencing
And his hands and feet are bleeding,

MARIE NOËL ~ *Hanging On In There*

All the sheep are following,
Trotting through the gap,

Into the meadow of Good Hope,
To pasture on day's upland stair
Where hooves that suffered bruising
Are soothed by love in flower,

Where bleating lambs are suckled
On milk from the pastor's heart...
Shepherd! Shepherd! blackest night
Is walking up my frightened path.

Shepherd, the narrow way to life
Will be cut off, the evil one
Is stuffing it with thorns, while I
Wander weeping, ever on,

Ask at random where this place is
That I knew and now is gone,
This food, this living water, this
Wine, this bread, this Jesus Christ...

Seeking healing, I go looking
For this passage...Shepherd, come!
Join in the dances, marrying
Your wounded feet with mine,

Give me your hands, all cut and sore,
Lay them in mine. Come quickly now,
Hold wide open heaven's door, allow
My little ones—and yours as well—

Their fleeces wet with strain and sweat,
To enter in and rest in glee...
I am the Sorrow of the World,
Shepherd, will you marry me?

WEEPING OVER THE MULTITUDE

We hate you

You who come up by night, calling down thunder on my head,
And in all the public squares hatch plans to see me dead;

You, bred in the east, new, armed, violent and intent
On uprooting the crop grown in time's soil, from grain of my bent:

Who efface the path before me where I might have dared to walk,
And parch the world I dwell in, drop by life-saving drop;

Who censure every mouthful of the bread that I eat
And, stick by still-flaming stick, tweak the wood from my grate;
Dismantle flower by flower my garden, my house stone by stone,
From that spot in humble light which was happy and my own;

You who, greedy for possession, knock out of my hands
The book I drank from daily and gain nothing for your pains,

Take it! Yours from here onward be land and roof and book,
Yours too the sun and shadow where I shut my eyes to look.

Take and eat the bread that's been my staple hitherto,
Take and eat your fill of all the words I—maybe—knew,

Take my worldly goods, they're free and given without measure,
Greedy hands will never grasp the riches that I treasure.

I give them to you weeping, you who trample on my pain
But will never force an entry to the realm where I reign,

Nor carry off the treasure that you filched in the dark,
Squeezed tightly in the anger of your unforgiving grasp:

My heaven on the high slopes and my tread money-light
Climbing up, my swift-winged hardship and my careless delight;

My tenderness that a flight of birds carries far away;
My gentleness, and the soft wool the four winds take to play;

My heart like a warm fruit speared by August through and
through
Till it bleeds for the thirsty...And the love I have for you.

Alas! All my riches that I toss around so lightly,
You are missing out on them, you who've robbed me too slightly.

Having eaten my dinner you will rise unsatisfied,
And from the book that slaked my thirst you'll go back dry...

I weep for you...You will walk out of my burgled home
Empty-handed, bare of foot, tattered clothing on your soul,

O you who will not get to feel the love that ever wells
Through my country's stones, nor my joy in the open fields,

You who will never reach my fount of living water,
O you now setting off down this lost alleyway of hatred.

PATHS II

The good news is proclaimed to the poor

We'll be taking the common paths, for we
Are common folk, and so we always will be;
By paths that Love has made its own, we'll go
With the two feet we've got—poor feet and daily.

God the Unknown, of neither where nor when,
The faceless God who lies beyond our sight—
Among us, only star-led Mages find
The door that opens onto his dark night.

These wise among us, when they've banged their heads
On heaven's bright shining, clamber daily higher
Up the stairway of their thoughts, watch for
God's coming on the roof-top of their tower.

Borne up from cloud to cloud they soar so far
Above their heavy, earthbound eyes, so high
And now so distant from their trusty feet,
Bared to the boundless perils of the sky;

So high, so upright lashed to the mast of reason,
In weather sundered from the seasons' round
And in a light that needs no other sun,
Their thoughts will come together all in one.

And where night throws itself into the arms of day,
Truth, which can marry yes and no, will show
Them—wordlessly—its name, its simple name.
Truth they will see there; Love they will know ...

But we poor shepherds who have nothing more
Than feet on stony sheep-tracks here below
To lead our flocks, that they may graze upon
What little they can nibble as they go;

We who hold nothing but a simple staff
To test the uneven path stretching before us,
How can we get a grasp of Truth among
The frenzied clouds above, the wild wind's chorus?...

We'll be taking the common paths, for we
Are common folk, and so we always will be;
By paths that Love has made its own, we'll go
With the two feet we've got: poor feet and daily.

God the Unknown will lead us on a way
That passes through our workshops, townships, ploughlands,
God the Unknown, dressed in a heart of flesh,
With feet like ours, and words to say, and hands.

Those who are Kings will hoist their wits aloft,
And come to know Love as the Truth he is,
While we who bear our burdens on our backs
Will do as Jesus did when carrying his.

We who are bad at marshalling our thoughts
Will follow Jesus in the flesh he wore,
And pass, day-labouring, through town and mart...

And with that flesh we'll find Love at our door!

It's through our hands that we will meet with Love,
We whose eyes see only chinks of daylight,
And with our fumbling fingers we will break
And share our bread, hands have no need of sight.

Our feet will find the shortest route to Love,
Unlike our heads which read road-signs reversed;
It's feet that serve to go down to the well
And draw up water for a neighbour's thirst.

And with our hearts that never learnt their letters,
We'll come upon Love as an infant frail,
New-born and fallen from heaven on the hem
Of night's black shawl, and lying wan and pale.

And like a baby swaddled and asleep
That still can't focus nor yet say a word
We too will carry, close-held in our arms
The Truth that we have never understood.

Then Love will visit our benighted want of wit,
Whispering Truth to us from door to door;
While crystalline Truth aloft will tell of Love
From depths of blue to Mages on their tower.

So be it. Amen. Thus will learned Mages,
Along with shepherds unschooled and ill-shod,
Their flocks in tow, arrive one eventide,
In the same place, at one in the same God.

We'll be taking the common paths...

Le Rosaire des Joies

VISITATION II

Magnificat

Elisabeth sits spinning in her open doorway,
—Eyes and ears alive to the distant sounds of dusk—
Here up the path comes the footfall of her cousin,
Mary of Nazareth, coming because she must.

Mary's drawing near now, heavy with the tidings
Of what's happened to her, in her, just weeks ago.
Seeing her, Elisabeth runs out to greet her,
Letting drop her loose thread for the breeze to blow.

God knows what they have to tell one another
Of such great urgency ... yet of a sudden all
Talk dries up: an inner joy sets them both trembling,
And silence envelops them in a wordless shawl.

Each seeks within herself a needed assurance
To confide to the other without more ado,
Here and now in words this hope beyond hope. Can it
Be true? And what if it weren't? My God, where are you?

But now, without warning, the miracle has moved!
Souls and bodies felt it, the silence was shaken.
The two of them, young girl and aged woman
Quiver: each to each their little ones have spoken.

O God! it is impossible, a waking dream...
It cannot be! And yet more real than any thing,
Even the sun we see. And Mary's heart leapt up
To sing, just as the may-tree glories in the spring.

She takes off, she rises, she is now in full flight
And, soaring through pathless space, arrives at the feet
Of God. There she sings, freed from earth's gravity,
Lost to time in depths of blue at the apex of height,

And distinguishing nothing, neither truth from lies,
Real from unreal, logic from folly, sense from nonsense,
She knows God can do All and a son shall be hers ...

Here's Zachary now on the threshold of utterance.

VISITATION III

Holy Family

They spend the time beside the window, flowers
Peeping in...Elisabeth, turned towards the light,
Pulls from her basket a piece of embroidery,
Linen, wool, and thread, in practical succession.

Facing her, the Virgin Mary who has keener
Eyesight, sews with tiny stitches swaddling clothes
And wraps, and little bonnets trimmed with lace
That she tries out on her fists for size and shape.

Her cousin as they work offers quiet counsel,
And Mary opens an obedient ear
To the care that infants at the breast require,
Her heart though is endlessly singing songs.

Her heart is spinning, spinning her a roundelay
A hidden tune sweeter than any yet heard,
To weave round the child fast asleep in her warmth—
It's the long hem of love that she's stitching now

Without lifting her eyes—or just the time it takes
Her to shift her work along without a thought,
And smile at the old man, who looks at them mutely
After each verse of Scripture, as he reads to himself.

And if one of the two reaches out for a pot
Needed from the workbench and looking heavy,
He notices at once and in spite of his age
He urgently goes over and prevents her.

The household takes its rhythm from time's slow pacing,
And as the hours slither one into another
The three barely hear peace softly purling past them:
Dawn waits on evening, and dusk dreams of day.

Paced by the clock stitching its dial in gold thread,
The women settle early to their work,
Making haste to start, to finish, and to start
Again, yet never managing to make an end,

Till eventually evening, wound in a veil
Comes slyly creeping into the house, and dims
The whiteness of the linen they are holding...
On the horizon loiters a dream of ploughing,

And, hearts heavy with the weight of hope they carry,
Mary, Elisabeth and her good old husband
Go to sit, the three together, on the doorstep,
Filled with shadow and silence, hands on their knees.

Far away, filmy fields fade into filmy sky:
Its crop of golden stars will soon be flowering.
Elisabeth, tired, wonders if she's feeling pains.
They look at the evening, dream, wait, and wait again.

CANDLEMAS

The good folk and their destiny,
Holding their candles tight,
The good folk and their destiny
Leave before morning light.

As they go out they carry
The flame within the wax,
As they go out they carry
Their souls enrobed in flesh.

The good folk of human kind,
"Where does the road begin?"
The good folk of human kind,
Find the path and turn in.

They circle round the choir,
Their candles burning bright,
They circle around God,
Who gazes, Light on light.

The mother walks upheld
Bearing her sacrifice,
The mother walks upheld
To present the child.

She is bringing the fair fruit
Of her maiden years.
She is bringing the fair fruit
Of a night's hard hours.

The father in his hand
Weighs the gift to be made.
The father in his hand
Has the price of some bread.

Old woman who have nothing
But the child of another,
Old woman who have nothing
Take him now from his mother.

The greybeard tired and shaky,
Whose feet won't obey him,
The greybeard tired and shaky
Walks beside her praying.

To God who is unable
To make a man alone,
To God who is unable,
They bring their very own,

The blood they have given,
The work of their dust,
The blood they have given...
The son they hold in trust.

They bring the child in flower
—Brief the joy to follow—

They bring the child in flower
That will turn to sorrow.

The child they must nurture
To see him grow tall,
The child they must nurture
To watch him die for all.

The good folk on their road
—the day has barely dawned—
The good folk on their road
Circle with lights in hand,

And slowly make their way
To God—the flame quaking—
And slowly make their way
To God—the wax wasting.

They pass beneath his gaze,
Every light a-flicker;
They pass beneath his gaze,
Their livelong day no quicker.

And God, the priest eternal
Whose rite doesn't alter
And God, the priest eternal
Steps down from the altar,

To take there from each hand
Wax, wick and flame away,

Takes the candle from each hand
To serve another day.

God in the feeble half-light
With wind from his lips blown,
God in the feeble half-light
Snuffs them one by one.

And nobody knows where,
Since God has blown them out,
And nobody knows where
The souls now go about.

Chants et Psaumes d'Automne: SONGS

THE ESCORT

To the church we bring, Lord God,
—since this is where you chiefly dwell—
Bring you, with the cross ahead,
One who has died. He needs your aid.

Ah! Jesus Christ! Ah! Jesus Christ!
Come to the aid of old Guillou
Who so lately, soaked in sweat,
Set off…where he had to go.

Today—no sun or sky for him—
He's in his coffin deathly quiet,
His feet so still, his eyes unlit,
Despite our candles shining bright.

We walk behind him with bent heads,
But so deep-dug, so dark the place
Where from today he'll lie at rest,
No torch will brighten there his face.

To travel to this dread abode,
Against the cold we dressed him in
His woollen socks and, hoping it
Would be enough, his better suit.

We've closed him in a coffin too
—In case of rain—and in best style
We've draped it for the route and borne
Him on our shoulders up the aisle.

But Jesus Christ, ah! Jesus Christ!
He's leaving now his last safe house
And we can't follow farther, where
Death takes him next is out of bounds.

Jesus, Brother, God and Man,
Alone you see, alone you know
The lodging between world and world
Where the deceased must surely go.

You who have travelled beyond death,
And know the way from shore to shore,
So that it took three days, or less,
For you to go and come once more,

Come to the aid of this good man,
Of Guillou, who today sets forth
On this his dark adventure, come
To meet him and to take him home.

Help him to feel and tap his way
—using your cross as walking stick—
And so come safely to that world
Where lie the pastures of the blest.

Best you take over now: the end
And final goal being still unsure,

Here where the escort changes route
We leave Guillou to your care.

Farewell, Guillou, forgive us, friend,
For leaving you in sad alarm
To face God's mercy on your own,
Farewell, Guillou, old chap, fare well.

Weeping we take our leave and go,
We've called on Jesus to come by...
Try not to worry overmuch
About your journey, nor shall we.

It may be he has been already,
Come and gone without a trace
While we were singing Agnus Dei,
To take you with him to his place.

DREAM AND SONG IN THE SNOW

1. Dream

To give a moment's respite
To the child dying in her sleep,
Angels slipped a foolish dream
Into the heart's dark keep.

She who expects no visitor
But death this Christmas Eve
Has gone off with the angels
To the Land of Make-Believe.

The angels have softly opened
The pale door to the yard
That she may hear the footfall
Of her love from afar.

The angels came in quietly
With a gold ring for her finger
That she might wed this very night
Him who, faithless, loves her.

When she heard that he was coming,
In her dream she smiled,
And as her love drew closer
In dream she was healed.

But when this friend, long absent
Would have kissed her weeping eyes,
She cried out and with pain-filled hands
Pushed him from her side.

Fleeing in tears, safe in her arms
She bears, past startled wingtips
Of the angels who beguiled her,
The soul that woke her up.

2. Song in the Snow

Angels who lead me astray, you mistake your gift,
Angels who divert me from my roads. The name
Of my happiness, even the nurse who suckled me
Does not know where I go when at dusk I shout it,
Too late, out there, somewhere
Where God has shut the door.

My happiness dwells where my living friend has his
Abode. I circle round it like the winter wind,
The great wind that comes begging, driven by blind
Distress to the foot of that dear dwelling-place
Where lodges the peace
It will never reach.

Home of my friend where he dwells in his love, while I,
Snow of the white and wandering hands, immense
And alone, envelop him in my shawl of silence;
Too timid to knock at household doors at nightfall

Asking for shelter, I falter
And lie on the threshold.

Ah, I never will share what pertains to the child
And to the belovèd, the warmth of the hearth.
The wind waits outside...It cries too much. If its breath
Visits the living-space, it will make the flames wrath;
Should it blow in the grate,
The fire will go out.

Ah, I never shall know how soft that nest is,
The snow must not cross the threshold so blessèd
That guards the door. Taking flight and now lost in
Its storm, it will chase itself through measureless space
Till time hides its fall
Once and for all.

But on this holy Eve I draw near the dark house
Where my friend keeps his Christmas, that I may see
His joy shining out through the cracks in the door
So intensely sweet—I can't look any more,
My hurt is too great
It might kill me straight.

So heightened the joy that is mine here this night,
So warmly I'm quartered out here in the dark;
Dear angels, the house my cry brought to your sight—
Guard it like a mother,
And wall it with wings:
I weep. Keep it safe. I haven't another.

SONG IN THE WIND

The wind is streaming away, it carries its crying child,
The wind is off to hide her far away in its homeland,
The wind which both earth and the sky have betrayed
Has left them behind and is fleeing to its own land.

It flees through the hills, leaves them quaking behind it,
It torments the wheat fields and flees through the rye.
The small church in the stubble gets down on its knees,
Vowing vainly to pray for the wind as it flies.

It flees past the meadows, the mere and the moorland,
Dives deep in the measureless sadness of dusk
Beyond the black woods, where none ever enters
And the echoes all die before they reply...reply...reply

It flees to a place no longer known, and there,
Somewhere, in the cloud of its anguish, prepares
To cradle and lull, dolefully and half-heard,
Its child who must die of the grief that is hers.

There, breathing so softly that no leaf is stirred,
It soothes its child with a long, muted moan,
and sings her to sleep in this soft undertone—
The child with the hurt that can never be cured.

But there in the undergrowth, see, hunters lurking!
They've set out to search for the nest of the wind,
Climbing up on the heights of the harsh table-land
Where narrow paths, childless, die out where they end.

They would seize for themselves in the solitude
Of that rugged land its secret. Aloof and wild,
The wind uses all of its many rough hands
To keep faces barred from the space round its child.

Its screaming hands hinder the hunters' approach,
Turn them round on their heels. It raises to fight
Them a desperate wall of wings fiercely beating,
Goes off, recruits itself, returns multiplied.

It hustles the woods on them, rushes in, shrieks,
And scratches their eyeballs with holly and yew,
The branches now whipped into fury it uses
To beat back the nosier seekers in view.

Their blind advance loses its footing, founders...
The wind flees...it carries through time's empty years,
In the half-torn folds of its mantle, its daughter
Sorrow, site of outpouring of evening's sweet tears.

It flees, fluid and streaming, where none ever finds it
Nor ever arrives at the nest it's defending,
Where, far from the earth and the sky and under
A cloud, it broods on the child and its dying unending.

Pale wind that sweeps over my unsmiling homeland,
Sweep me up in your crying and lose me with you,
Like a bird in a far-away silence, small, nameless
And living but partly, that nobody knew.

Won't you take me and hide me? I too am fleeing.
When in a dark wood I was singing, the path
Of the hunters swerved suddenly to pursue me.
They are saying they want to see my naked heart.

It's the nest of my soul that they want to capture.
But no one will find it—unless one, maybe—
They will hear the chattering magpie demanding
That plenty of space round the limes be left free.

They'll amuse themselves there with songs and suchlike,
But none will attain to the far and faint heartbeat
Of the brotherless child, our own, ours alone,
She who is gentlest of all, our sad sweetheart.

She who trembles so much that she can't be heard,
So tender that should one, just one, make a sound
In the leaves where she's quivering still, a mere
Glance would suffice to inflict a mortal wound.

She's my little child who's been taken and broken,
The sobs of the wind bring her back to me here,
Where she finds no solace this evening, whom vainly
I soothe in a heart that is darkened with fear.

Don't let anyone else come near her again,
Wild wind! Wait until she has slept for a while.

Not a single one. Hedge her round with dark wings...
Do you hear me, wind? Not a friend, above all.

Don't let anyone ever puncture that sleep
Filled with muttering darkness and dreams distraught...
Above all, not a friend! There's nothing that weighs
Like the merest brush of friend's foot upon heart.

Chase each and all paths from the field of her fretting,
And the sky and its clouds too; her friend though, so
Gentle—wave him off to the world's end, but fondly...
A final adieu ...that won't quite let him go.

Whirl him up in your draught, implore him and take
Him through lands great and small, that never again
May he come back to find me wiping the tears
Of my child who will never be healed of her pain.

Useless nurse, here I sit, my arms round a child
Past all hope of healing, intoning a lay,
With weary voice broken and blurred, to help pass
The time without end she is taking to die.

SONG ON THE RIVER BANK

The river's running is unending
Flowing onward, cool and gone,
The one-way stream has taken vengeance,
Yet I don't know what I've done.

In my two hands I was holding
A heart I never knew was mine
Light as a breath between my fingers
Or as fluff blown on the wind.

How came this gentle heart so promptly
And so late to my shy hands?
Hands worn dry by autumn bluster
Let it go with the wind again…

The river swollen with love's grievance
Hurried comes and hasty goes,
For ever elbowing the verges,
Where it seems my fault arose.

Along the stream I seek my trespass,
To weep for it and wash it clean,
But in the tall grass by the water
There's no finding it again.

The heart that flew to me, so tender,
I loved it so, where is it gone?

I never dared to take and hold it,
Barely touched it save in song,

Fearing to be my own deceiver,
Think it mine, and with a squeeze
Wake it, and watch it as in dream
Turn *other* and start shedding leaves.

I held it by a thread...but barely...
The wind can wear those through, it's said...
Or else, trembling through nerves and joy,
Maybe my trembling broke that thread.

Thus did I lose that heart's belonging,
Like her who trips at dusk one day
Dropping, ah God! her son, her treasure
In the current hurrying by,

Into the water that won't listen
Deaf to the cry that bids it bide,
That water running, running faster
With my lost love in its tide.

Year-long I run beside the river
Trying to catch up...Time and sky
Both keep their counsel. I peer even
Into the breast where the heart once lay.

All I see is a man quick-marching
Getting away as fast as he can,
As void to me as my name is hollow
To a voice that queries who I am.

The river's running is unending
Flowing on, for ever gone,
The stream in flight has taken vengeance…
Tell me, water, what I've done!

WILL AND TESTAMENT

I leave to those who shared my living space
My years of toil in body and in mind;
My path that has the end in view and heads
For it, unfaltering and never turning round.
I leave them too, lit with the light of day,
My face, fixed in the calm that practice has
Perfected; my smile as well—it has done valiant
Service—my clear eyes which have never wept;
And my hard heart they knock against in passing,
A heart so hard it can put up with all it gets.

To each of those whose soul I had to carry
On top of mine down the long road to peace,
I leave herewith the peace that I have earned
Day in day out, and doggedly amassed,
My heart's wealth scraped together, at much cost,
All of my peace that they may have enough.

To those I count among my friends, I leave
The patch of sky which God placed in my soul
And which I found without seeking permission
Snug in a fold of my astonished
Heart while earth's round back was turned.

This too for them: my cache of joy, concealed
From all the well-trod paths of Time; that is,
The new-born infant that I bear inside me,
Who opens his eyes when nobody is looking;

His artless feet that move—and are my songs—
When in my heart we dance to them together;
Our feast days and the pictures that we treasure,
And the unlooked-for wonder of the Mages'
Star, which, rising, wakes and leads me straight
Into a kingdom in the dead of night.

Another legacy for them, the limpid spring
That fills me with a sudden gush of water;
And the occasional genie that I meet with
Unforeseen; and the Angel that I saw;
And the good Lord who passes in my prayer,
No sound, no footfall, just a light; the word
He uttered, wrapped and veiled in silence,
A word spoken so low I hardly hear it,
But which on re-entering the world I bring
To any I find waiting at my door,
The faintest breath, a waft of Holy Spirit,
Which they will understand if I have missed it.

To my friends, that hope may grow in each,
I leave to all—I do not know to whom—
To all, the good I never worked for
But which I have received from God our Father,
All the joyous grace which secretly and at
Rare times in time he gave me graciously,
That they may keep it in my stead when in
Deep darkness it has left me all alone.

And last of all, to you who are a stranger
—yet deserved a better portion—I leave...
Nothing...the harm and hurt I harbour, all
Of it. To your heart's door I know no way,

I have no key; I'll always be kept out.
Vainly to that closed heart I leave my inner
Dark of soul and body, my truth that I have shown
To none, my times of gloom, the pitch-black paths
I wander down, the thoughts that twist the hands ...
The danger, deaf and mute, that hems me in,
The great pain so intrinsic to my being
That if I ousted it, I'd leave myself,
The pain that seeks and finds me where I am,
The pain of being an exile in the world,
From which, so close to you—and yet so far—
I'll perish...leaving you the echo of a cry
That circles round unheard, and round again,
And cries...and the poor tenderness that lies
Within, in a lost Eden now unvisited.
To you I leave the inner wound that dares
Not answer in the open to its name,
Which asks for nothing other than to die
With no word said and beyond pity's reach.
To you I give my fault without a face,
My livid shame, my heart held in contempt,
A heart so weak, so feeble that a single
Passing smile was once enough to shatter it.
To you, the passer-by who from the brink
Of autumn was to smile at me impromptu,
For this smile and, dear God! for all the good
It did me, now that I'm leaving, all I have
To offer you is the wrong in my life,
The harm that I have brought into being
And which will die without my being forgiven,
My poor wretched wrong I entrust to you alone...

But it's to you that I have given the most.

THE FACE

When I stand at the last, Lord, at your door,
Like one returning from a long day's toil
Still wet with sweat from the dire trial of dying,
Tired out with fast-days and the year's pain and moil,

And when you want to change for a face of glory
—As a child is changed into its party dress—
My faded features worn and scuffed by time
And place a crown upon my head—no less:

When your choice is hovering between my ages
—Springtime of girlhood, winter white with snow—
Before the godliest of these times of passage
Is immortalised as clothing for my soul,

Don't give me, Lord, the appearance of a saint
With solemn lips and eyes swimming in light
Looking calmly down on fires long snuffed out,
Nor the angelic air that prayer sometimes brought.

But summon rather from among my guises
The down-and-out girl in the tattered dress
Going nowhere, lost in wind and storm
On a foundered road and far gone in distress,

Who, in desperate need of food and lodging,
Trails down an autumn path in ugly weather,

MARIE NOËL ~ *Hanging On In There*

A track that none ends up and none sets out on,
And where no door is opened, nor hand either...

Her young cry filling the dusk with tenderness
Sees the sky veil its face in self-reproach,
The horizon echoes her lone cry of distress
Till, life taking fright, death begins its approach...

Recall out of time past that weeping woman,
That girl in rags with no looks to commend her,
Desperate to find a way out of a world
Offering nothing that will feed or mend her.

Call her back, shaking, her mouth grimed with tears
For all the grief and horror that she's lived through,
And bring her home again with wet hands hiding
The shame in her eyes, of which nobody knew.

Weak as a child left without any food,
Sad as a sin that no one will forgive,
Repellent as a leper defaced by his scourge,
Or as decay in the dying who still live.

Remember the moment, the place on the road
Where, struck by a lightning bolt, this prey fell straight
Into evil darkness and bled, drop on drop...
There, the one who was passing, late, oh so late,

Met her. There he who was climbing through the storm
Took pity. Simply he took pity. Nothing more...
It's the face I had when I looked up at him
That I would like for my beauty on that shore.

Flightier than flame, more fleeting than a wing,
I wish it, ever as pallid as that day,
To be, in the dazzle of salvation's dawning,
The scared face of my everlasting joy.

Chants et Psaumes d'Automne: PSALMS

DESTINY

As my life drew near its noon,
With a basket in my hand
I left yesterday at dawn
To walk across the land.

I am off to see September
Where an apple tree awaits...
You can leave the door ajar,
I'll be home in two shakes...

As I left, our house was saying:
"Be sure you come straight back!"
The sky is clear, I'm taking
Just my fair-weather hat.

As I passed the church's face
Where blue-eyed shadows crowd,
I slipped in to say a word
Of greeting there to God.

"Father," said I to Him, "I trust
That You will hold me good-
And-tight this day till fall of dusk,
And He said: yes, He would.

Up the dead-straight way I went,
So smooth and sheltered is it,
It wouldn't trip the smallest child
—even twist its foot a bit;

And without hesitation
Or fear the way were awkward
I took the faithful path that knows
Every single orchard.

In that garden I set foot...
—Peril unforeseen, unheard—!
There I came upon my soul
After noon when nothing stirred,

And as in long grass, hidden quite,
A well may yawn and bare its throat,
So my soul loomed there agape ...
And I fell into its night.

ILL-MET

They had kept it hidden
Far away from me, my soul,
They had kept it hidden...
I had never looked at all.

For they had placed across it
To keep the door shut tight,
For they had placed across it
The Cross of Jesus Christ...

And, over that, the virtues,
As strong as any steel;
With chains around as well,
Colder than winter's chill;

And on top rules on rules
And prayer upon prayer,
For who knows what last straits
Are held at bay in there?

But today go out and play
Dear child we have watched over,
It's time you took your chances,
All's out there to discover.

Go alone into the wood,

Little girl in our care,
And pick if you should find them
The berries that grow there.

Off you go, our little saint,
To the secluded wood
And see if the dove is there
That makes her moan to God;

Go to the leaf-dark wood
Where you'll meet no other soul,
But do not ever walk there
Naked in your own.

For it's a wide, wide land
And filled with misadventure;
A land of many paths,
And all peradventure.

On the first day of summer
The girl I was went forth
And walked into the wild wood
Down an untrodden path,

Alone with trembling heart
And both my hands uncurled,
And only my white veil
To shield me from the world.

And as I walked through morning
Down the woodland glade

I met the thyme in flower,
The pansy and the sage,

The honeysuckle too,
Small roses jubilant...
"If my soul is here, I said,
It's not on my account..."

From one of the top branches
A bird called out to me.
"If my soul is near, I said,
I'm not to blame, not me..."

But as the day passed noon,
Behind the sneaky reeds,
What sinkhole deaf and dumb
Has mired me in its ooze?

What was the wind that blew me
Into my soul?—This dew-pond
Is my soul?—sad and sick to death
It lies there moribund;

And sins in the foul water
Swim with glazed eyeballs,
Amid wings flapping wildly
In ugly, loathsome brawls;

And from the depths a cry
Of a woman wailing—
An angel pleading refuge
From the beast that's prowling;

And sins on the surface
Go floating belly up
Over remorse unshriven
In midwater's livid lap;

And a crime from the bottom
Comes up to show its face...
—The name I do not know,
The spelling is d-i-s-g-r-a-c-e.

And in—or maybe outside—
Lies a faceless body,
Fruit of dubious vengeance,
A tale hidden from me;

Another nameless body
Lying there, still as death,
Like the fate awaiting me
Since the day of my birth;

And underneath the flood
Lies Death with staring eyes,
And feet drunk on the blood
Drained out of human lives;

And in such fetid water
As low tide leaves, submersed
And appalling—God, turned back
To front, his face...reversed.

God, Black, Almighty and Alone!
His, the mill the One Law turns...

All the world's blood is seeping
From underneath that stone.

Oh, all you good believers
Passing by, men, women, all,
Stretch your saving hands to me,
And save me from my soul!

Save what's left to me of heart
Still beating in despite
Of mortal dread, all aghast
At the horror of the sight;

Save, for a few years longer
And some mileage on the way,
This body that has little
To inspire the light of day;

Put back in locomotion
For the daily journey
To take her to her death-day
One who's dying already;

To ensure she dies in winter
And a long way from us
Let us close the staring eyes
Of the pit with long straws.

To bridge the ghastly mouth
Agape with endless horror
Let us throw some wood criss-cross
—Dead sticks—before tomorrow,

So that, too scared to look
At the yawning hole down there,
At nightfall the benighted girl
Steps on it, hands in prayer.

And we will all pretend
As she crosses over
And tries this trembling arch
That we believe the cover

Affords a solid bridge
Where a foot can feel safe,
A ground that's firm enough
To bear the weight of life.

SONG OF THE GUARDIAN

It is here that I wait, sitting where the roads meet,
The angel who unspools the strange thread of the paths,
Like a mother I sit here, ever listening out
For the soul that has wandered off on human feet.

Here I sit, waiting, stooped over pitch-black Night,
Waiting until she brings me back the docile steps
Of my little girl, having first made her drink,
Her head under foul water, from the noxious pit.

Here I wait for you to come back after school,
You whom life overlooked when the right time came
To teach you, when the grass was growing tall,
The luminous experience of the spring.

You who have as yet learnt nothing of life's day,
Of how noon waves farewell to morning's brief bliss;
Virgin in vain, did you think, face turned away,
That you would be saved from Fate's lacerating kiss?

Were you going with a closed mind to sail down
The years, playing nursery games still unaware
That your God, whom as Man you lovingly gaze on,
Has behind those eyes a cliff-face dark and sheer?

Children find it hard to say goodbye to childhood,
But if a flower can't resign itself to see

Its blue, defenceless heart both die and decay,
How then can it hope to ripen its own seed?

Oh, my child, be docile and do not run away:
You will die and decay, God allows and we follow...
I who love you and weep for you, have myself
Led you, like some meek lamb, to this very horror.

Night, who will be teaching you, runs a harsh school
Subjecting her pupils to abuse and shame,
But some of the saints who once endured her rule
May have won there the new, the God-given name.

Be pliant, my child, and abandon control
To that mistress of the dark you rightly dread—
When your heart is wallowing in inner murk
Like a drowned body in its watery shroud,

When you find that your God has ceased to defend you,
No longer giving you a thought or a look,
You'll be left with nothing but learning your homework:
The word Amen, the only one in the book.

Say it and sink. Swallow all. Swallow even
The abyss where the sky now reversed engulfs you.
Sink, with hands folded...the apex is there
Where the sky, turning turtle, re-enters heaven.

That done, you'll return from black Night to the world
Like a babe emerging from a vast unknown—
Drunk from imbibing a surfeit of deep light
And crying, looking up at the lightning of God.

MARIE NOËL — *Hanging On In There*

You will come back bearing a weight of distress
For day on the wane and the falling of night,
You will come back freighted with tenderness
For the sons of flesh and the daughters of blood.

You will come back a woman who's learned the cost
Of tears like all mothers grown old in grieving,
Of wiping men's eyes and kissing their hurt, and
Being for them the poor sister they're needing.

You will come back from school, pale and weary, head
Heavy, your eyes sunk and reddened, trailing along
The thin streaks of dawn where the first bird is flying—
You will barely make it to where you belong.

And there between lilies and garden fountain
I shall be waiting, who love and watch over you,
And shall have kept for you, fresh as yesterday,
Morning's blue milk to remake the child in you.

I shall place on your plate for your simple tea
An apple and pear, and butter and honey,
And I'll wash your dress, and will pour you to drink
Before falling asleep a glassful of sky.

Should you take your time to return to God's house,
Put off by the sheep-track, so narrow and bare,
That leads grazing ewes to the uplands, take heart,
I shall fly to meet you and carry you there.

STORM

This is my hour; this is the Reign of Darkness[1]
Luke 22:53

Now comes the hour...the adverse hour...
Dusk is falling,
Around our home whistles a wind
Black and appalling.

And O my soul, my only child,
Who lie there dying,
Night enters, hand-in-hand with fear,
Where you are lying.

This is the hour when angels wage
War up above;
The Evil One takes vengeance on
The God of love.

They are fighting out the battle
Of fate versus fate;
Now heaven that protected earth
Has doused its light.

1. The quotation is significantly incorrect. Here, in St. Luke's Gospel, Jesus is addressing the high priests and the exact words are "this is your hour..." The fact that an obvious error has been left uncorrected, suggests that it was a deliberate alteration by the poet. At this moment the High Priests were doing the devil's work, Jesus had been handed over to torture and death, the domain of the devil, and in Marie Noël's day, this would not have needed unwrapping.

And in that fray the forest fights
For life and limb,
Twisting and dishevelled, howls
Its battle hymn

While from a chapel close at hand
A bell's heard ringing,
Its pale voice raised in "Save Our Souls"
Above the gale dinging.

My child…! her lamp is on the floor…
Alas! my poor child…
See! the good path that misled her
Is now running wild,

And hope that rocked her in its arms
Lulling her to rest
Has been upended by the dark
In a flash.

She has no God, no Father, no,
Nor ever will
Have roof or door or heaven. Here…
There…she wanders…till,

Has she gone mad? Or is she dead?
On one great cry,
To the farthest tip of anguish
She's borne away.

In the gale her soul keels over
Sinks and is lost

At twilight, like a sailing ship
In the sea's dark breast.

Birds on the wing that mock the roar
Swelling below,
And in foundering light swoop and
Soar with the flow,

Yesterday my dear was naïve,
Simple as you,
Holding her eager hands out to
The sky's soft blue.

Oh, my little April girl, so
Blossom-white,
Our family-God's—the Father's—
Precious pet.

Alone in a grieving world,
Alone at dusk,
Swept in a frantic whirl of leaves,
Hope a dry husk,

She's caught by autumn on the road:
The Unfamiliar
Who puts the skies to flight is come
In search of her.

At nightfall sprang the Wolf, the Male,
The One Accursed

Out of the vast wan solitude
To do his worst.

The one who'd had his eyes on her
From babyhood,
He who lies in wait for children,
Even the good;

He the Strong One who in nightmares
Groans aloud,
Rolls his outer pelt of shadow
In sap and blood;

The Prince of darkness, who sets up
All human fates,
The sin of man and woman,
And death that waits;

He, like some long-drawn eerie howl,
Grisly, inhuman,
Drives the world to lunacy, He,
The Evil One!

Evil that at every birth
Lets Time in,
And in the heart of innocence
Skulks unseen;

Evil in all human homes
Waiting to pounce;
Evil, Time's out-liver and its
Forebear once.

Evil before Adam *was*—causing
Him to fall,
Evil ripe before Eve saw an
Apple at all.

Older than the Knowledge-tree,
Light-bearer, he;
Black Lucifer, not light but dark,
Self-willed so to be.

Evil from before all ages
And of after;
He that has, save secretly,
No father;

Evil, dark elder son, with no
Known beginning,
In darkness behind darkness
He took being.

All you good folk, so snugly set,
Just tell me how
This poor little soul of mine can
Recover now;

Where will she find healing, today
Or tomorrow,
Who saw deathly night and swallowed
All its horror?

MARIE NOËL — *Hanging On In There*

How will she sleep, this sickness in
Her very blood?
How can she trust in God to work
Her any good?

God...! Ah! my little dove's afraid
Of Him today.
She's falling into this abyss
Where she will die...

Dead already? Mad maybe...?
That vile angel
Bearing her, could he be on
His way to hell?

Where have morning's Angels gone,
The dawn parade,
Who launder in blue the swaddling
Clothes of fate?

Where were they when autumn's Evil
Came to get her?
Where went God, when he abandoned
And forgot her?

Vainly rings the angelus in
Heaven, now bare—
None to help her, none to listen
Not one to hear.

None above, nor in a world laid
Waste; no, not one

Left to people her dark night,
One and all gone.

Not even you, sweet Virgin, with
Your heart so blue;
No Saints to pray to, not a candle
Standing true;

Not father, mother, soul that breathes,
All are too wary,
None will ever follow her
To Evil's eyrie,

Just I alone, my little soul,
Of all that throng,
In the open, unprotected,
I and my song.

I, who am alone the nursemaid
To your sorrow,
Rocking on the precipice your
Pain and horror,

Singing, to the storm that no one
Cares to quieten,
A song to help it sleep until
Morning lighten.

A song to dull the torment
Of the hurt unhealed,
Sung at the peril of my soul,
My only child!

OFFICE FOR A DEAD CHILD, I–VI

A voice is heard in Rama, lamenting and weeping bitterly
Jeremiah 31:15

Psalms of Rachel
It is Rachel weeping for her children
Jeremiah 31:15

I. Funeral Train

The child so fragile born to me,
Lately we took him out to see

The world, walked out with him
Into the gay sunshine of spring;

In young May carried him between
The fields dressed joyfully in green;

Into the town with friends and kin
Deeply asleep we bore him then...

In vain the bells along the way
Rang out, in vain they had their say,

His eyes tight shut, he slept so fast
That he forgot to wake at last,

Even when passing through the square
Amid the people gathered there.

… … …

Others in church on that today
In lieu of me cared for my boy.

Over him first the verger spread
A coverlet, white with silver thread.

The priest sang next to welcome him,
Two choirboys piped up for the hymn.

And last of all to touch my child,
The gravedigger who laid him mild

In a new cradle deep below
Against the wind that likes to blow,

And threw in earth to be his quilt
And keep from him the coming chill.

All that was done was for his good,
And each one did the best he could

To lull him and find words to bless
And shelter him from night's distress.

Each did his bit...and now they're homing,
Leaving him to what's surely coming.

Oh, hurry away! Be gone with you!
The hour of darkness is here now.

The dusk is falling, time you heeded
Your own children where you're needed.

Go back home, and thank you kindly...
It's my choice to stay here blindly.

With my boy I'll sit it out,
Wait for the cold and for black night,

For I'm afraid in that deep bed
He won't be safe or comforted.

I'll wait in the dark, I'll wait right here
To find out if he's crying there.

II.

An angel came to us on Friday
To suffocate my little boy
And take him off to Paradise.

Despite the springtime rent with cries,
And his breath in its great fight
Entreating God from dawn till night;

Despite the sweat that soaked him through,
The window with its eyes so blue
That opened to let in the air;

Despite the air that heard him dying
And to help him started sighing;
And the milk with life to give,

And water saying: drink and live!
Despite the gentle wool that wants
To share its warmth with him and can't;

Despite my hands that love in vain,
Fussing on the counterpane
Against an ill whose hour has struck;

Despite the women on their knees,
All fingering their rosaries,
And sobbing softly: "Pray for us";

Despite the other Angel, bright
And spry—his own—supposed to fly
Around this earth and save the mite...

From all danger bar the only.

An Angel, stronger than the other
Is come my tiny child to smother.

Is it difficult? Is it right,
For an angel spared all fright,

To squeeze to death, like some white dove,
The trembling heart of the babe I love?

That heart with time still chock-a-block
(And God himself had wound its clock),

That would have loved a rocking-horse,
—And not a year had run its course—

All the long night it beat...it beat...
To save the seconds as they fleet;

All night the heart went battling on...
At daybreak, lo! the Angel won.

And the child I failed to mother
Turned reproachful eyes another

Way, to the unforgiving sky
There to address his plaint on high...

His eyes then swivelled in his head,
Veered suddenly toward his God,

God unmoving, black and awesome;
See me he neither could nor would.

III.

Behold, O God, the knees I bend
Rest now before you on the ground.

And here too, Lord, are my poor hands
Vainly in prayer before you joined.

And my own voice that trembles so,
Reciting prayers of long ago,

The words come readily to mind,
The meaning though is hard to find.

Lord, You are God, and naught am I,
I know this well and say it high.

It's your right as Omnipotent
To take back gifts that were just lent;

As God, it is your right to be
In the right when grief strikes me;

To You, the strong, I can't deny
The right to doom our sons to die.

You are God, You are great,
The One who does, and so may take.

You are God, and You are good...
Indeed You are...No! shouts the blood!

Again I try—to get it out
I say it with my eyes tight shut.

I say it, but too low, too far
For my soul to overhear.

I say it, but the heart I had
To credit it, is dead, O God.

MARIE NOËL — *Hanging On In There*

The hands that I held out to you,
Somebody has cut off the two.

Eyes that I kept raised to heaven
Have been darkened, blinded even.

Were it a man who'd done me this
Most dreadful hurt and slept in peace,

Were it a man, under the blow
I'd go and seek refuge in You,

And You'd avenge me, God most just,
Were the murderer one of us.

But if it's You, what can I say?
Bad is good and yea is nay.

It's a dubious kind of bliss,
A godsend one would sooner miss:

Being God and fearing neither
God nor man, nor asking whether

One need give account to any
Of one's dead and living many.

There's nothing so great or so good,
Nothing like being you, O God!

But better not to undergo
The fate of creatures here below,

And be down here the whereupon
You exercise your mercy on.

IV. Credo

By reason of the lime blossom
That with gentle living pity
Soothed one evening my child's terror
As he left on his last journey;

By reason of the poppy flowers
One of which chained up his hurt
In a compound walled and dark
Where the pain at last fell quiet;

By reason of that air the kindest
Of old women sang in vain,
As he came to breathe his last,
To calm his fear of the unknown;

By reason of those on their knees
Who watched the whole night at his side,
And of Our Saviour, God made man,
Whom pity for us crucified.

By reason of His cross, borne too
By others bearing hurt for hurt
And pain for pain for pity's sake,
I believe deep in my heart

And say to You with muted breath,
You who subjected life to death,

I believe in the awful Good,
Sublime, that can't be understood.

V. Prayer

Fatherless Father, never man
Nor child,
Who know not, seated in peace,
The evil that life wreaks upon
The living.

Father who have no body and
No blood,
Who know not, black Innocence
The evil death wreaks on the dead
In passing.

Father who have no heart at all,
Pure spirit
Tearless, painless, fearless, call
To mind Your Son our Saviour, who
Suffered all.

Learn from him the agony
Of dying,
And the great pity and the crying
You should show to the misery
Here below.

VI. Deo Gratias

The nuns in their enclosure
Mantled by the living God
Have finished singing Vespers
Curtained from exposure,
Far from cities and their bustle,
Far from human pain and hassle,
Far from wails of Woe! Alas!
Have sung: Deo Gratias.

But even as their voices soared
Together like one forest bird
Higher than treetop and its nest
In the clear blue air to rest
Perched in heaven's infinity,
The pale strain broke in splinters,

Falling like a nightingale
Hit by a stone as sharp as hail,
Falling ever low and lower,
Falling ever slow and slower,
Heavy with cities busy buying,
Heavy with people direly dying,
Feebler, weaker, note by note,
As it might be drops of sorrow
Falling from a broken heart
On the feet of God most high,
Trembling with tears—alas, alas,
Falling: Deo gratias...

EVENING HYMN

O Lord my God, here comes my eventide, light fades
And dark is on its way
To nudge me—not far now—towards the pensive grave
Where there's no more to say.
And I seek your hands before my lips are sealed in death
To kiss them for the gifts they gave me here on earth.

Blessèd be you, Lord, for my earliest weakness,
My body's many ills,
Whereby a painful bolt got pushed home on all doors
That opened to the hills...
Here I found my cloister with many a quiet chapel
Where I would light for you my one and only candle.

Blessèd be you, dear Lord, for the plain-Jane face
Which brought me little honour
And proved too meek when seeing a passing happiness
To grab it by the collar...
Had it been pretty, had one made of me his queen,
Would you still have come and loved me, God unseen?

Blessèd be you, Lord, for this house of false promise
In which my days ran on
Devoid of flower or fruit or child or merriment,
My nights loveless and long...
The bird of heaven took flight there in its shadow
And all the country round was comforted and hallowed.

Blessèd be you for my neighbours, that thorn thicket
Growing all about me;
And for the darts left in my journeying heart
By nearly all who passed me...
For it was in the worst stretch of this endless mile
That I received from you, for all of us, a smile.

Blessèd be you above all for my feral season,
The summer left unspoken
When the nights' growling thunder wreaked in me a havoc
That left me badly broken ...
For it was in the deepest dip along my darkest path
That a dewdrop fell from heaven—O wonder!—in my mouth.

Blessèd be you, Lord God, for the life that is mine
And will soon be passing.
But for death which is coming and I do not trust,
I give you no blessing.
My eyes which it will close have never yet descried it,
My body doesn't know of it and my soul denies it.

It is indeed a nasty and shameful piece of work
Made by a baneful hand,
Carelessly cruel and callously disgusting,
To defile our end,
Yet not by you, O Beauty offended by each part,
But by some limb of Satan from the everlasting pit.

And yet since in the past your graces have all come
From some mischance of fate
To delight my heart with a spray of startled stars,
Maybe death, come soon or late,

After doing its inglorious and sordid worst
Will turn to me a face resplendent as a sunburst.

Blessèd be you, Lord God! For all my misfortunes
I kiss your gracious hands.
And knowing not what I do, I kiss them for my death
In your tomorrow's plans,
Dear Lord, in whom I was the pale, barren and obsessed
And soon-to-be-dead woman—and in all these blessed!

Chants d'Arrière-Saison

THE ROAD OF NOT-TODAY

Down the long lane of Not-Today
That wanders far, while lost to view,
Walk I, a booby: better I'd
Taken a wonted avenue.

Down a wrong road footsore I plod
Carrying all I had of wealth
To a place where no-one wants it,
Holding it of paltry worth.

I kept this treasure out of sight
—And hidden thus may have it still—
Neither of silver nor of gold,
But flower essence for all who will.

I offered it to those I met,
But on the road of Not-Today
Where trails a scent of discontent,
Seeing my ware, they turned away.

From my own garden, for love's sake,
I gathered once in girlhood's hour
—Sweetly scented, purest colours—
All essences of that one flower.

Secretly to him I tendered
This heart, this rosebud, closely furled...
In May picked and in May proffered,
Turned down in May by all the world.

Then like a woman setting out,
Weary before the day's half done,
To glean what's left of summer's grain
And feed her children while she can,

I harvested in wood and field
The wisdom that the seasons hold
And the Chant of Ember Days
For children I left in the fold.

I had this grain, and fruit galore,
Sweet water drawn from well to cup
To foster life in flesh and soul—
The children turned their noses up.

What a waste of time and toil—no
Hoarder I, so I've no merit—
To work all day at bringing home
A harvest no-one will inherit!

Oh, hard it is to tramp day-long
Arriving at Mad-Market Square

Offering gratis love and bread
To find that none is hungry there!

Rain falls. No light on the horizon.
It's the wrong road ... just do your part ...
A carrion crow squawks mockingly
At the bread weighing on the heart.

But who's this walking, just like me?
Who is it, bearing such a load?
Walking the Road of Not-Today,
So wan of face? Jesus? You, Lord?

What are you looking for down here,
You and the Cross you bear in vain,
Where nobody gives a toss for it
Along this hard, uncaring lane?

If you were not our Blessed Lord,
—the best, the one without compare—
A down-and-out I'd take you for,
So tired you look, downcast with care.

What do you hope for, my poor God,
On this road with never a hearth
Nor soul who'll open up and take
The weight of love that breaks your heart?

Rain falls. No light on the horizon.
A black crow squawks non-stop in jest

At all the bread that's going stale
Dying of hunger in your breast.

On the vain road of Not-Today,
From dawn to dusk the rain has poured
Down on me without let or stay.
And even more upon the Lord.

Dear Lord, how would it be with you
If we two helped each other out
Like two vagabonds frozen through,
Before we push ahead tonight?

As weary pilgrims ease their backs
By swapping heavy haversacks
Might not our sore hearts find relief
Through an exchange of grief for grief?

Give me the grace that's big with pain,
The pining love that floods your heart,
That weighs you down and pricks you so.
Perhaps that will relieve your hurt.

And I give you with every step
The long despair that's on its way
More leaden now than yesterday
To throw my sad heart on the dump

That ends the road of Not-Today.

CLOSURE

When the years have rolled by and the evening comes
Where I, foot-dragging and faded, with drooping
Shoulders and reddened eyes, am now merely one
Old woman too many trailing around the house;

When the home that was mine and lovingly cared for
No longer concedes to me room or role,
When the new-lit fire and the burgeoning garden
Ungratefully elbow me to the wall.

When my very last needle has vanished for good
And all I can do is love under my breath
And cause my granddaughters minimal bother,
My beautiful girls, who would not mourn my death.

Then quietly I'll open the door at the back
Like a woman poor by birth and for life,
Who goes out to throw in the lane running by
The torn remainder of her ill luck.

Then, as the day pauses and draws to a close,
Like a stranger to all and who leaves all behind
Her…and then, like a motherless child whose cry
Has no place of safety to which it can fly,

I shall leave on my own with the age that I am
Which has long been devoid of song, charm or bloom,

MARIE NOËL ~ *Hanging On In There*

Alone I shall set off to meet with grim death
And leave in my wake neither discord nor grief.

I shall search for the meadow—the only one
Where a happiness, unknown to all other plots
In the country round, swelled the heart of the child
I then was—the field the haymakers forgot.

The field that got lost at the end of my childhood—
The woods took it off to their black secret heart
And walled it so high and so far off in silence
That no day-lit path has set eyes on it yet.

There grows the flower that has never unfolded
For any but me in the spring of my life.
Maybe here in this meadow behind the nettle
The dawn bird awaits me half-way up the sky?...

I'll step into the field without bouquet or bundle,
The lost flower and bird will be there before me,
I'll cloister myself in my grassy chamber ...
They only will learn the rest of the story.

Then, like someone reciting alone his last mass,
In this meadow that shivers and pales with a start,
I'll begin in a voice tailing off into silence
To sing the air that shatters the heart.

There I shall weep for my lovely lasses
To whom their gold years are now paying court,
And to bid them farewell without risk of recall
I shall love them then without limit or thought.

And there I shall weep as I wait for the ending ...
A caged turtle-dove as the sun goes down
Will moan a long time awaiting its freeing.
Day withdraws from a field one flower at a time.

The faint pulse of time which beats on in my heart
For some unknown reason, will step by slow step
Withdraw from the world, and the drooping leaves
That die with dusk...will, falling, cover me up.

OLD WOMAN

Old woman weeping in the wood
Follows where the shadow leads
Turns her back on hearth and homestead,
Children and their needs.

The months in the year's retinue
Have fled without a word,
Of the flower that bloomed this morning
Never a field has heard.

The trees in all the country round
Sleep, so old, so weary,
A single solitary leaf
Falls, so late, so dreary.

The crow goes flapping in the wind,
Belches a black squawk:
"Where, aged crone, all alone
In dusk's bane do you walk?"

"I took the farthest of the paths
In the last wood by the sea,
I am looking for a fountain
To weep there with me.

From what far tree is flying
The bird of the last day,

That it may give me comfort
On the passage that goes one way?

For I am called upon to die
At a time and place that wait,
And I am walking at this hour
So as not to be late."

THE LAST GRIEF

The great Grief turned up one evening
On the threshold scoured and swept...
She came walking down time's stairway
Bare to the wind and black of step.

Other little Griefs before her
Have already been and gone,
Those foolish little Griefs cried
To the four winds, one by one;

The little Griefs, still hurting, cried
Like children the night through,
The wind that sweeps them elsewhere
Dried their tears as it flew.

They had wept from dusk to dawn
And nothing stilled their cry
Until morning washed their faces
With the garden's early sky.

But the great Grief, the last of all
That follows on the turning years,
Silently, invisibly, one evening
Slipped into the house.

And the house which once was built
To keep the flame in the grate

And love leaping to meet it,
Grew chill and flickered out.

So dark the house, no paths will call
There now. It is too late.
The sky has run dry in the gloom,
The winds have blown their candles out.

The great Grief with her withered hands
Who will not weep nor yet succumb
To the hope of being healed
Of time's doom by time to come,

The great Grief, morose and dreary,
Sits beside a fire that's dying,
Sits there motionless and glum,
Grey head on her shoulder lying.

The house, forgotten and forgetting
Under the dead weight of the skies
Hasn't an open window left
Where it can go and change its eyes.

Too sad an evening to dislodge
This last Grief: there's no reprieve...
The house has no door any more
By which Griefs can up and leave.

VIATICUM

Listen, you who hand me water,
It's too late now...that time is past,
Gone is the body's memory
Of bread and wine, hunger or thirst.

Oh, you who take a cloth to wipe
My face, what is the use in trying
To wash incipient decay
From the features of the dying?

What are you doing, hands that hover?
All your efforts go to waste;
If you want to help this outcast,
Go and fetch me Jesus Christ!

Run and fetch Him in the wafer
Where He dwells now, oh, make haste,
Bring, and in my failing body
Sow, like a wheat grain, Jesus Christ!

The grain that must die utterly
And rot away to dirt and dust
Till from the life in wheat that's dead
New shoot, new ear, new life shall burst.

What are you doing, futile hands,
Agitating to no purpose

Round the abyss? Busy hands of
Last resort, now you are surplus.

Away and find his hidden door
And fetch Him for me, make it swift!
Hand Him over, candid morsel,
To share the squalid fate I'm left.

Matter with matter broken down
In the dark pit alive with guts,
Throw in the Host to rot with her
Who lies here dying in the dusk.

To sow in me a being that lasts
And to confound and foil death's plan
Throw soul and body this all-pure,
This morsel of the Risen One.

Throw, to be swallowed up with me,
Into the vast obscurity
Of the gaping mouth you see
The seed corn of eternity.

THE SPRING

All others are other,
Men, women—all,
Their hands flush with money,
Contentment, the soul.

As for me, I'm a Spring
In the wood of unknowing,
I'm the Water that's drunk
By none in its flowing,

The Water that gushes
From shade—a tenderness
Sequestered in thickets
By its distress.

Water born before dawn
So that in earth's droughts
Its limpid love
Might slake dry hearts.

I'm Water at nightfall
Still palely flowing,
Nothing to look at,
Just tears of imploring.

I'm the Water that ripples
Tomorrow as well

To please one who has drunk
Elsewhere his fill.

I am the Water vital and pure
Yet running to waste
Through purlieus forlorn
Where none cares to taste.

I'm the Spring that is fated
To fail at the last,
The weeping Spring that will
Always thirst.

A BITTER LEAVETAKING

Let me go on my way. I am leaving you
As I would a land where the streams have run dry,
Where fear-filled evenings can't find any doors
As they wander homeless and whimper and cry...

There was once—was it yesterday?—a child,
A poor little thing, of no use it would seem—
Born out of season and who knows where?
Conceived when her mother was in a dream.

She was not made for living, being neither
Pretty nor handy in anyone's view,
Not really real, just other. Her eyes,
What were they telling us? Nobody knew.

She set out to walk down her very first path
When he promised to take her to the well ...
But instead of a drink, it was a washout
She met when she got there, and laced with gall.

She was always stumbling in the half-light,
Ever more tolerant of passing hurt,
And gave, without uncovering her face,
To him who never looked at her, her heart.

She walked throughout the day until it died,
Ever more orphaned, held at a remove

As much in the warmth of vain assemblies
As in the ill-jointed commerce of love.

She's tired to death. She's in pain. She is leaving.
.. ..
If you go to the world's end to seek her out
Where the friendless field is dousing its light,
There'll be nobody there. It's now too late.

Should you go looking for her in Heaven,
The maid-of-all-work will be there to find:
She did her best to ease human distress,
The task that her Master, God, had given.

You will meet again too the girl who served
As everyone's sister ... no, not the one
Who hadn't a brother and falters now
In the mislaid place that's been seen by none.

Let her be gone. God knows where and how
A great offering will be made of her
With silence as her only chorister.
Let her be gone...
I am leaving you now.

SONG OF THE ROBE

The King had given me
When winter's wind blew raw
The King had given me
The seamless Robe he wore.

It is the Robe of Love
No tailor cut or patched,
It is the Robe of Love
None but an Angel touched.

It is the Robe that has,
Of soul immortal spun,
It is the Robe that has
No flaw under the sun.

The King gave me his Robe,
That I might wear it too,
The King gave me his Robe,
Blow wind, come ice and snow!

It being the Robe of Love,
Nor wind nor sharpest hail
—It being the Robe of Love—
Will pierce it or prevail.

The King gave me the Robe,
But took it back again,

MARIE NOËL — *Hanging On In There*

The King gave me the Robe,
And then returned it torn.

"Without my robe of Love,
My Lord, what shall I do?
Without my robe of Love,
Out in the rain and snow?"

He handed me some thread
—I fear that it may break—
He handed me some thread
To mend it for my sake.

I sit up late and sew
And with small skill repair,
I sit up late and sew
The pauper's dress I wear.

I've sewn so many patches,
Stitchery on stitchery,
I've sewn so many patches
With docile zealotry,

It will last long enough
—Stiffened by looking new—
It will last long enough
To see a widow through,

It will surely do me
Till leaves and berries fall,
It will surely see me
Through winter's bitter chill ...

But when the north wind wakes
And starts to make war,
But when the north wind wakes
Scouring sea and shore,

When the cold seeks me out,
Its breath searching my life,
When the cold seeks me out
With its deathly knife,

By probing stitch and join
Of my defective sewing,
By probing stitch and join
—Thread wasted and time owing—

It will find in my heart
The secret chink, the fission
That opens in my heart
The great Laceration.

MARTHA AND MARY

Martha, the elder, is so old,
She's toiled so hard and for so long
She's lost the use of arms and legs
And lies at leisure in her bed.

"Mary, is the dinner ready?
Are the stockings mended yet?
What are you doing that I can't hear?"
"Only praying under my breath."

"Leave your prayers, that will do,
Go and tidy up the house,
Time you went and fed the goslings."
"Sister, they've got quite enough."

Martha, aching from lumbago
Lies at ease on her plump pillow
Eyes and ears on high alert...
The day is long and time rings hollow.

"Who's that knocking at the door?"
"It's the doctor come to see you."
"Quick, let him in and run to get a
Liniment that will make me better."

"Who's that knocking at the door?"
"It's the lawyer come to see you."

"Fetch the ink, run quicker still—
I am going to make my will."

"Who's knocking at the door again?"
"It's the Lord who's come to see me."
"Tell him you can't take it easy,
Sit and chatter at his knee,

Tell him that on Saturday
You take the rugs outside and beat them
Tell God to go back to Heaven
Until Sunday afternoon."

"Oh, dear Lord, please go away,
I've all the housework nowadays.
Do go away, but not too far
So you can see what I endure."

"Come, Mary, come! For seven long years
I've called you and you deaf your ears!"
"I'll come—but please, a moment's grace
To have a cry and wash my face."

OUT AND ABOUT

Now, it fell on a Saturday,
At the third hour after noon
Which no clock struck.

The two white-haired women
Had set out round the town
Under the sinister blue sky
Digesting, drunk with death.
Round about the town they go,
The town that Fear has just emptied,
Leaving the streets drained of life.
Leaving the squares lying stretched out
Motionless on the pale ground,
Save at the focus of destruction
Where the flames are now at table...

The two white-haired women
Have set out to call for help,
Set out to ask for news, they're
Going in circles—the noon sky
Has just now killed the town—
Going nowhere through the silence
Of the streets. And the streets
Lead nowhere, square after square has gone
Missing—the sky that death fell out of,
Having nothing left to do, looks on—
They walk...No threshold hears,
No window sees, no door replies.

The flames are at table, eating their way
Through neighbourhoods to their hearts' content.
They devour their prey with relish
And no one bothers them...

Where are the guardians of the town?
Where are the saviours of the houses?
Where are the stretcher-bearers?
Where those who take away the dead?
Where? The relief has fled.
Where are the eyes and where the footfall? ...
They wander through the silence
Among stupid windows
And horrified doors.
Where is the footfall? Where are the eyes?
Where are the arms? Where the hearts?
Where are they? ...Only a girl in white,
Keeping vigil at the side of woe, is bent
Over the road's last cry.

Those still around since noon,
The two white-haired women
Under the ugly glaring sky
Find nothing in the silence
Save the vanished squares.

Then, at the turn of the third hour,
The third hour of Saturday,
The third after noon
Which no clock struck,
Then, in the ash-grey fear, then
In the irreversible disaster,

Then, in the frozen horror,
Then the enemies entered the city.

KEEPING VIGIL

The old house of our forefathers
On its ploughlands firmly founded,
The old house of our foremothers
By its garden snugly bounded,

The old house of our foremothers
Sitting from Easter Day to Whitsun
In its sweetly pretty garden
Sown by Jesus Christ, God's Son,
With flowers from his own domain...

Ever-watchful, penny-saving,
Ensuring measure and good order
In the back of well-stocked shelving
Where stored bedding—linen, woollen,
Waits on births and deaths to come...

I hear a knock...and now another...
Loud banging under the flagged floor...
Light the fire in the living room,
And the candle for the death throes
Of the dear house, blessed in years,
Soon it will be falling down.

The Evil one is come from Hell,
—the son of a false god made man—

MARIE NOËL ~ *Hanging On In There*

He is come, the bastard son,
To kill, towards the end of time,
In hate unsheathed the elder Son,
Pillage and kill at toll of bell
What's left of his inheritance.

To the House he is now come
With his pickaxe and his false hands
And the house, so old, so good,
By her chain held back the dog
—She would have gone and bitten him—
And the house, so good, so old,
And closed to none, said: "Do come in."

With his pickaxe and his false hands
He came into her very heart
And underneath dug out the grave.
Beneath her shovelled out the earth,
Undermining all four walls.
In the dark I hear—you, too?—
The pick—a blow—another blow—
A third—a sullen sound of falls
And debris slithering below.

Take the child into the garden,
And shelter it under a leaf
So a bird tomorrow morning
Can feed it from the branch above.

Put a light to the last lamp,
Pull up a chair to the last hearth.
Fetch the sheet and tablecloth,
Perhaps we'll still have time to darn

Them if we keep our stitches big.
Stand clear of the partition—look!
It's leaning. The windows' teeth
Are chattering...Can you hear?
I hear below, I hear the thud...
I hear the thud, I hear the soil
Losing its footing where the pale
Bed stands. Sweep the fallen plaster
Lying around the living room.
Try to underpin the tipping
Flagstone in that livid corner
There. We still have the time perhaps,
If we are quick—but hurry now!—
To restore order once for all...

Do you know which bird will come
And perch tomorrow on the branch?
Did you hide the child with care,
Fearful that some magpie might
Come soon and peck away its life?

How long will evening last today?
Listen—The mattock is at work
Harder...louder...closer...surer...
Faster...Do you hear the wall
Behind you starting to keel over?
And that dreadful door agape?
The threshold sinking? ... Now the roof's
Been taken ill—it's giving way!
Quick as you can—there's some bread left—
Get our last meal on the table.

Draw some wine, we may have time
To sit and eat there: still today
It looks as it did yesterday,
With the same lamp keeping vigil.

I hear—Ah! drain your final glass
In one!—I hear a sudden crack
Sneaking snake-like down the wall
Ceiling to floor. Now if you want
To check the time, see the last hour
Through the door, it's on its way, so
Get a move on! If you've business
That needs doing round the House,
The old house of our foremothers,
If you have something still to fetch
From the wardrobe or the bedroom
Or the loft, you'll have to run…
Is the stone already graven
For the house that's on its deathbed? …
I hear the dust that's falling from it,
Settling, now, across your shoulders…
It's time someone intoned the Psalm
—but will it make it through to morning?—

I hear the pick…I hear the mattock
And underneath, the yawning pit
Where the ghastly grave is edging
Close and closer to the hearth.
It's time to wake the passing bell.
I hear the pit…I hear the end…

What of the child in the garden?

THE LAST MASS

I. Offertory

Receive, O Father, on this altar
Set up here by us poor mortals
—low as it is, look on it kindly
From the heights that you inhabit—
Receive, O Father, from our hands
The sacrifice of human kind.

On this table to be offered
And to you made over, Father,
We've not laid the native fruit
That no human hand has toiled at,
Yet that ripens to perfection
All unaided while we sleep.

Take this, for it is Our Bread.
—As if, my God, you might know hunger—
Take in it the Suffering
Endured by all us human creatures
On our way from dawn to dusk,
And by the clods in every field.

Take, O Father, this the woe
Of man and beast, the running sweat
Of both at plough, loud shouting
As the coulter slices through

The clay…Within, our Bread, should
Frost-free Ember Days allow.

Bread in seedtime and at harvest,
All the turning year storm-threatened,
Standing between earth and sky
Like regiments marshalled for wars,
And, in the stackyard crying out
As grain is beaten from the ears.

Our Bread. Strain in the gale-blown sails
Stress in the millwheel's mighty splashing
Toil in the sacksful borne by men
Weighted down like beasts of burden.
Pain of the wheat so fiercely ground
Under the millstone round and round.

Our Bread. Hard-fisted Suffering
Is quick to groan twice over,
Once in the flour bruised in the kneading,
Then in the baker bent at labour.
Groaning too in the wood stacked high,
Sawn and split to feed the fire.

Take the Bread we bring you here,
Father, and accept besides
An offering that costs us dear:
Indeed no higher currency
Have we to render you each day
In homage for our destiny.

Receive here "Father" on this altar
Not the Godsent drink that falls

As largesse from the sky above,
Nor the sweet spring water running
Ever from its hidden fountain
Without care or need of us.

In the morning's chalice poured
Take this Wine we offer, Lord,
Take it, for it is our Pain
Of days and weeks, and more again,
As still, back aching and bone-weary,
Body bent, we shuffle forward.

Our Wine. Climbing up the scarp,
Mattock searching round the vine roots
Yard by yard from vale to ridge,
Ever wrestling in an armlock
With the unseen mischief-maker,
Be it canker, frost or grub.

Our Wine. Innocent flesh and blood
Of grapes, crushed in the dark heart
Of the vat: an unjust act
To which every bunch falls victim
When the sweet juice runs at dusk,
Squeezed to death by vice of press.

Father, receive here in kind
The Pain of life in bread and wine:
Side by side we sweat in throng,
Through drag of years and age unstrung,
Until the reaper comes along
And scythes the sinner with the sin.

Deign too, deign last and most of all,
To take, dear Father, from my hands
And those of others of like kind
Who've drawn no living from the land,
Sorrows borne alone in darkness
Poured now in the common chalice.

Receive, more valiant still than Bread,
Toil without fruit, hope without yield:
Who sows free seed in heartbreak field
Gets no harvest. Take instead—
More punishing than toil of slave,
Scourging, fire or millstones—Love.

Receive, more often poured than wine,
Love whose well-head never fails,
Love that gushes from split rock,
As common water spilling out
By night unnoticed will then spend
Itself in the uncaring sand.

Receive the heart which never yet
—Even beaten, heavy-laden—
Wearied of its wailing burden.
The mute heart of the shouting hours
That rises to the passing moment,
Dies without defensive comment.

And accept from it the heart's-blood,
Poured as pardon, ever flowing:
Mercy, source of tenderness
Come from evil in another,

Now floods out upon the altar,
Greater yet than sin that's mortal.

At the first mass of the dawning
Take this human Host and offering
—Pain of Bread and Pain of Love,
Pain of past relived this morning—
Frail and docile in old fingers,
Paid as due in love and suffering.

Yet given that one of ours once walked
Among us, and that one was God,
Your son, Father, ours as well,
Bare to the wind that blows on all
—Man from that first infant breath,
As Man he breathed his last in death—

Receive the Host we bring today
Humble like us and high as He,
Speck of dust and fruit of thorn
Just as we are, and yet divine,
But no less God than you are, You!
And in this Host accept us too.

II. From Benedicat vos...

Blessed be those who in their ill-lit rooms
Would offer me a refuge never found
Elsewhere, poor nameless folk of a poor town,
Needy folk without mastery or means,
Who have but little bread and that paid dear.
During my dreary years on the long road

Where I went wandering, my heart mislaid,
They sheltered in their pain the stubborn hurt
Left over from my girlhood vain and void.
And having lacked life's staple, they and I,
We drank together from a common cup
Of misery. In deathbed they brought me
To birth and mothered me; small as I was,
They in their turn, weak as they were, without
Return, became my children out-of-hours,
Turned into my Sunday daughters, were my
Easter sisters and my brothers singing
Every Christmas in the parish choir, and
In joy and anguish we walked hand in hand,
Their hearts in mine, and through tough years when theirs
Was the one kiss flowering in the desert
Of my soul. They warmed me at the firesides
Of old women, they loved me, they, the simple
And the true, just as I was, no fame, no flower,
When nobody noticed me, they loved me,
They loved me! O my God, love them in turn!

Chants des Quatre-Temps

THE DUMB GIRL'S SONG

The Daughter had a lover
Who came knocking at the door.
—Lover, O lover, may my angel hold you up!—
The Daughter had a lover.
The April breeze was turning the heads of them both.

The mother took a look at him,
Young and poor and trying his luck,
—Lover, O lover, may my angel keep you safe!—
The father took a look at him:
"That cheeky chap, he said, has a big appetite."

They turned the lover out.
"Go and sleep with the maid!"
—Quick, lover, off with you! Stand proud, but hold your tongue!—
They turned the lover out.
The Daughter lay down on the step: "Over my dead body!"

The mother trod upon her heart,
The father trod upon her mouth.
—It is only a bitch that lies down on the ground—

The mother trod upon her heart.
The house-door banged shut with a mocking laugh.

"Daughter, have you lost your mind?"
She has swallowed all her love songs
And walled up all her chatter in her soul.
"Daughter, have you lost your mind?"
From that day on she never spoke a word.

She is working, thread by thread,
A story all in lace
With towers, bridges, windmills, chapels, travellers,
She is working thread by thread,
A tale without an ending but a deep and subtle sense.

"Daughter, here is your intended,
This notary who seeks a wife."
Embroidering she follows a pattern in her soul.
"Daughter, here is your intended."
She's embroidering the moon and gives no answer.

The father to the doorstep goes:
"All in vain I toil and scrimp,
My poor little holding will end up with my neighbour."
The mother from the doorstep wails:
"What do children bring one save bitterness and grief?"

When embroidering the sea
—Her hair was ashen-grey—
Think of days upon days that pass without a word,
But when the sea was finished
Her hair was white as snow that falls in winter.

MARIE NOËL ~ *Hanging On In There*

The mother who no longer sees
Shouted out: "Give us a drink!
I'm thirsty, I'm hungry and I'm frightened of this dark."
The father who no longer moves
Tried to raise his stiffened arms towards God's sky above.

"Here's some bread, here's some wine,
Here's a plate and here's the candle."
"Answer us, speak to us, O my dearest daughter."
—Here's some bread, here's some wine,—
"Speak, heartless girl—a mouth fed to no profit!"

"Old people, here's the candlestick,
Under the door you'll find my mouth,
My heart is in the place where the bitch has her bed,
Old people, here's the candlestick,
Take a good look at the soles of your shoes."

I DO NOT KNOW

I do not know what I possess,
Nor where I can unload the lot,
Hurry, good Friend, come to my help,
Take good and ill, take all I've got:

Happiness filled with such distress
As will break the life I hold;
Misery filled with tenderness
Such as mends the worst of roads.

I don't know if I anger you
Dispossessed, or please you rich...
Maybe my tears have more appeal
Than another's smiling face.

I know not—it's for you to know
Whether I can be dear at all...
Or if I'm worth another's love...
I know not...I'm a gift, that's all.

A SONG OF HIDING

Close my life with Your well-oiled key
As You would Your private garden within the walls,
And when those people come to summon me
To sew or cook or do some pointless task,
Say to them: 'No, neighbours, sorry, no.
The soul who was within, I've taken her away.
By all means go inside—by the stove,
Near the well—look for her if you like."

Hedge Your secluded plot with holly bushes
And plait it round with brambles, thorns,
Gorse, nettles and cow parsley.
If I am there, my neighbour passing by,
Try as he may, will not see where I am.
He'll walk straight on without pushing the gate
And I shall be behind it in the sun
Like a flower grown knee-high next to You.
Take and conceal me in the latent wood
Where all the birds are hidden in the leaves,
There, my winged heart poised upon Your finger,
I'll sing for You should You but wish me to.
But when those people, filled with pious zeal,
Come to find out which branch—as if it were!—
This nightingale is perched on in Your heaven,
You'll say: "She's where the moon shines blue,
She flew off at my bidding."

A BIRD

The ploughman, his donkey, wild oats in the plain
And the wheat that he sows conspire to make bread…
A good-for-naught bird with nothing to do
Flutters by on its way through the pathless blue.

Mankind walks too low to catch as they go
The hearts that hover between earth and sky,
While God with the net of his mystery
Tries to gather them in, but he is too high.

Hesitant hearts afraid of the holy
Float as far from the earth as from heaven's fire.
A bird, good for naught in a ditch or a hedge,
In a dark treetop sings higher and higher.

A bird flitting nowhere will draw them after
From leaf to green leaf, still spilling its lays,
To a glade, maybe, where breathes the one flower
Which has to be picked on this day of days.

A bird with its birdbrain, that knows not the goal,
May lead them yet through a series of heavens
To somewhere so blue and so pure that it could
…if only…be just the beginning of God.

SONG OF THE GIRL OF LITTLE WORTH

She was one of many Marys
Found growing nearly everywhere,
Whose birth is registered one day
In a town hall who knows where...

She was one of many Marys,
A little girl of little worth,
Her mother lying underground
Couldn't nurture one on earth.

One dark evening—she was singing—
Someone took her in his arms,
So dark was that moonless night
Perhaps he never saw her charms.

What did he say, what did she hear?
Nothing maybe...maybe all.
Does one know where words get blown
When the wind is playing the fool!

A heart, no face, brunette or blond,
By the hand he led her off.
She went to the world's end blind,
Never saw the path they trod.

He got her to join in the dance
In the square where fun was had.
She danced her way around the world
Without hearing what he said.

Till one day the sun looked brighter
In another pretty place,
Taking a new road he left her
Lost in time, alone in space.

Those are flittings one can pardon,
These are faults that will get shriven
In a girl of little worth, who
Wants, herself, to be forgiven.

Slowly, quietly she's gone back
To her unnamed place of birth
Where she'd stumbled into being
As a girl of little worth.

Takes herself, a humble presence,
Careworn feet and folded hands
To sit, her eyes awash with silence
Where the roadside Calvary stands.

And there—come joyless sun or rain—
She waits—how long? A life-term's tough—
Waits for time to finish passing
Down a road that's had enough.

But pale with dust or hoar with frost
Will come the day when she must go

The common way and then the Friend
She had and lost will never know.

That's best! To trot out empty words
And turn others inside out
And dressed in mourning, what's the point
For one not worth a passing thought?

But may a woman, one who prays,
Will it be me, or maybe you?
Say a Hail Mary for her namesake,
The girl who wasn't worth two sous.

CHILD'S SONG

Look at the pretty garden
That God gave us this morning,
All bright sunshine and flowers
With many-coloured eyes.
To keep it safely in its place
We've built high walls around it
To stop it running off at night
Where we would never find it.
And with our biggest strongest key
We've locked it up behind a door
In case the Wind, that boisterous thief
Should blow and blow while we're asleep
And take it for a rubbish bin
To keep his pile of dead leaves in.

WHEN THE DOG ROSE OF SUMMER

When the dog rose of summer will be but a thorn
And a hip on the hardened stem of the briar,
When the leaf no longer springs green, and the root
Is inert in the sodden soil underfoot,

When the wind which played at harassing the hills
Has dropped flightless to the desolate ground,
When the heart that loved me is lodged in the breast
Of an old man stiff as an ice-bound pond,

When for him I'll retain neither bloom, song nor charm,
Nothing that speaks to his ear or his eye,
When for me all I'll see is an old, dry-eyed grief
With a stale aftertaste of yesterday,

Then the hour will have come, and it's here at the door,
To sweep up dead years and to empty the grate
And tip the lot out through the postern gate,
Out of now, out of here, in the deep without floor.

THE DESERTER

He had a homeland all his own
A saint in white from head to foot,
A soul he'd only ever cherished
On Sundays, face-to-face with God.

Yet she remained his own domain,
His rich soil, his golden grain,
His truth, his troth, his limpid rill,
Where noontide stoops to drink its fill.

Loyally he'd served his lady
As a squire waits on his lord,
His life a candle at her shrine,
In duty pledged to One adored.

But now there blew a fitful fever,
A pestilential summer bane,
Corrupting between heart and lips
The truth that runs along each vein,

And, through foul water slowly seeping,
Below the flow it rots the reeds,
While in the air now rendered squalid,
Birds drop singing from the trees.

He walked on in a blur: a lie
Denaturing his private space

Has bred false twins from unity,
Planted a forked tongue in his face.

He walked farther: faith keeled over,
Found no footing in the marsh.
Then came on underbelly sliding
Through the grass the snake—or worse ...

He walked on...the past had gone,
Tomorrow sank in the abyss,
Now gleamed malefic in the gloom
The slant eyes of the basilisk.

Seeing his homeland with him still,
Back he came and sat beside her,
Softly sweet-talked her, as though
He'd not a thing to hide from her.

As though still in honour bound,
He filled her ear with what was false...
She meanwhile had bent her pallid
Head, the better to hear worse.

Round the two a shifting leeway
Offered him a choice of ends
Where every path embogs itself
And all the highways go round bends.

His homeland was ever present,
Lake of mercy spilling over,
Flooding the decaying verges
Where the muddy rushes wither.

Silence unbroken by a cry,
Bare feet, bare hands, and in white dressed,
There she was, his place of being,
And he beside her, baby-faced.

Keeping that same face wiped clean,
He stepped out of his summer sky,
And trampling on the spotless robe
He turned and left her, high and dry.

APRIL'S DAY

April had a DAY laid by for me, as secret
As a bud still green.
None knew what April would coax from its unclosing,
Whether fair or plain.
 The roses bloomed,
 The grapes glowed red.
More radiant than rose and richer far than wine
The day that April gave me outshone any seen.

On the same April day when you, April, passed by,
Old, I come again
To seek once more the tranquil DAY you left to be
My heritage ahead.
 But from month to month harried,
And ever more wearied,
April down the years had run so fast and so far,
And the weather had so changed that the DAY lay dead.

And so I went away on my little girl's feet
Alone to the Lone Wood
To pick wind-blown anemones and violets sweet
For weaving a shroud.
 To my knees I dropped
 And recited pray for us,
Then dug out of the earth a bed snug and soft
To lay to rest the DAY whose beating heart had stopped ...

When the days re-enter the everlasting blue
On the DAY of the Lord,
—those which on earth, being the most pure and true,
Outshone the larger horde—
 You, then adorned
 With Spring new-born,
You will be April DAY, crowned Blessèd Saint Tuesday,
And seated next to Easter DAY in heavenly array.

ALLELUIA

All has passed: April's flowers,
The flower of time, the flower of age,
The Star that once traversed
A fading sky, where are they now?

Advancing step by step towards
Dark night, the weakened foot has lost,
In losing track of this and that,
Its very paths through memory.

But in the dark where chance's Star
Shone true and fair from first to last,
Soars up from this returning day
The Alleluia of the dust.

SWAN SONG

She is there, alone, where the road peters out,
Too weary to reach a dusk wearier yet;
Filled with threadbare grief and the dying echoes
Of cries, there on eternity's doorstep she sits...

She is there...night falling has draped her in shadow.
Under her two crossed hands she presses the treasure
The day has left her—the long wound kept ever
Open in the same heart by the same bitter love.

She is there...The town around has unmade itself.
The hours around are no more than an ending.
She is there...searching her soul, then turning to read,
Were it written, the name of the way she has taken.

She is there, looking back at a far-off land, to
A wounded time, which stone by stone she ascended,
And, like a child drawing near to death, to the hurts
Borne in silence, again and again, unmended.

Down years and through blood, offences and cruelties
Hot and glacial have drained away...Sitting there
She remembers, recalls them, and with her veil wipes
The poor sinning feet that trampled her on their way.

Forgiveness comes flooding, flowing from her sad eyes
On Evil that neither place nor age have drained dry,

But the Evil ahead, which nothing now resists,
Lifts its angelic mask and, resplendent, smiles.

1963

INTRODUCTION TO THE GREYHOUND

O inconsolable death of every animal ...
O gaping cry of the human animal
O cry emitted as the end approaches
By the flesh...
                O great cry of the God-Man,
When, on giving up the spirit, he bowed his head.

God is not the subject here, nor could He be.

This is an objective poem on the following theme: the gradual withdrawal of space and time from the consciousness of the being, human or animal, as death draws near.

Following on the *Consummatum est*, this is the supreme moment of the "great cry" preceding the *emisit spiritum*. Then it can happen that in the fleeting ray of consciousness which forms part of the final passing, the last sigh of Love is breathed out.

THE GREYHOUND

The greyhound is stretched at the feet of his Queen
Very old, very tired. He looks without seeing.
But now, from the evening behind other evenings,
One approaches in silence, gives barely a sign.

He gets up and goes—"Greyhound, whither off?" A wordless
Master has given an order that takes him away.
All is forgotten: the house and its doors and even
His name, its calling lost in the lack of reply.

Unaware of all round him and deaf to today,
Which shivers in grass uncertain and fearful,
He pads softly along. He acknowledges none
And none in the fields sees him pass. He's soon gone.

He moves ahead steadily. What point in haste
When the place that will meet him will come when due?
Passing through fields where no flower is left blooming
He comes to the lost field where dogs go to die...

"Wait for me, wait for me, Greyhound! I'm ready.
I have let the years fall from my yesterday's hands,
The long, weary travail laid on me is done,
Let's be gone, you know the way, let's be gone!"

I had on my famous dress, and laid it aside
(Keep it, chambermaid, wear it too if it matters
To you): to walk in the wind of my dishevelled hair
The dress I shall need is the one that's in tatters,

The one I wore sweating, chief guest at the banquet,
The night I was racked by a chant in my ear
Till I drained to its dregs the cup of black wine
At the hour when friends are asleep in the garden.

I'm ready, I've pulled on my worst pair of shoes
Where dust has sucked up the complaint of my soles...
To follow you, pale hound, and lose myself with you
I need here and now every one of my wounds.

Away with these roses! Away with all flowers!
I'll take only the bleeding posy held tight
To my heart, made of arrows and thorns, so that
At my side its right royal crimson gleams bright.

Nothing adorns my warring flesh as this wound
Does—and that one, and that, and another here.
I had thought to close them, kneeling beside them
And, with angel aides, keep them soundly asleep.

But back they come now. And in force. The whole lot.
And no one this evening with strength to restrain them.
Come along, let's go...They are all returning
From the dark cache of my day, to throw me out.

Let us go where the world has no refuge remaining,
Where earth, under a sky grown now unseeing,

Slips away and gets lost from one end to the other,
And where, house by house, the town totters and falls!

And down they go, place after place, those keeping pace
With us and our haggard feet! And die, time, die!
Let us go to our singular meeting with the hour
That has none to come after, not one—let's be gone!

Let us go! And should I, as wearier, be first
To fail, your ear will maybe then catch, my friend,
The most desperate of the cries that aren't heard...
Let her die who must. You, carry on to the end!

But in the dark into which you're descending
With all yesterdays that expire without trace,
If a chance wind should take you via the place,
Now dim, where I wept for hope at a dawning,

And if he reappears who once made me Queen
In exile's vast kingdom, should your ways cross unplanned,
Just half-turn your head toward him in passing,
Feebly and sorrowfully, and lick his hand.

WHERE AM I GOING?

Where am I going, Soul, through Death,
Where walking without my human feet?...
Did I know it, Soul, when I was born,
Or when the road without a signpost
Took me from the shadowy field
Left shivering in morning's chill,

Did I know where I was being led
By alien years that counted me
Through living into dying,
That I might be tried and tested
Far from my homeland, widowed
Of the One who uttered me?

Not knowing the source I come from,
Soul, nor the goal of my hard journey
Through day-labour, this single
Mite of truth is all I hold:
A Son of Man has guided me
From Father-Love to Love.

Where am I going?...The world's
No more; lost on the sea's deeps
Beyond the last island, I hear a loud
Soughing, an all-enveloping murmur:
Love, my veiled homeland, where faceless
And timeless the Love that is God
Awaits me.

IN CONVERSATION

M. N. asks lapidary questions and leaves them hanging on a thread of silence over the abyss.

THE ABYSS

This passage of prose poetry might be said to open the *Notes Intimes*. In fact, Marie Noël chose to place first an exchange between the soul and her creator, beginning: Lord, Lord, what do You think of my songs? Its almost childlike tone, the reassuring God it introduces, seem strikingly at odds with what follows. Before. After. Two states of being, which frame an event, a gulf that yawned in her life, the Abyss: on the far bank lies her girlhood, prolonged by circumstance well beyond the age one might expect, on the nearer is her life as a woman who has undergone a physical, emotional and spiritual breakdown from which she emerged slowly but wondrously whole. Her *Notes Intimes* offer a commentary on the sweep of this life, broken and yet whole: her poems are its incarnation, blown on the wind of the spirit.

Les Chansons et les Heures

The *Chansons* were the bursting into song of a young woman who had grown up wound round as tightly as Epstein's Lazarus in an unsuccessful effort to "fit in," to please all around her, including God. Suddenly she found a way of escape: she could sing what was in her heart, while hoping that nobody would understand. But it didn't altogether cure her fear of offending, so she wrote the slim collection of poems entitled *Les Heures*, treading a well-posted path railed in by piety, the personal disguised in Sunday best:

> I wrote them in a few months. Then I went back to my beloved "Chansons."

It was only in her "Songs" that she could be wholly herself, tell her own hidden truth, sing at the top of her voice in words and, often, music. And so she would, year by year, the voice never cracked.

WHO AM I?

This poem, chosen by Marie Noël to open the door to what would become her life's work, defines what she already understands as central: the conflict at the heart of the person she was. In her twenties she clearly perceived herself as two people. She would discover later that her God was two Gods, which was even more frightening. She knew that the solution to the paradox lay in love, but was as yet unsure of what form that love would or should take.

On view too from the outset are the gifts for expressing, shaping and helping to resolve this dualism: her rare intelligence, self-understanding and sensitivity.

SEWING SONG

> "In the evening, when I'm all alone in the fields I sing traditional songs." (*N. I.* 53)

> It was in those years then, between 1902 and 1905, that I gradually found the poetic form I needed—what might be called the traditional song or ballad form—for expressing my inner truth without handing it over. In these songs I yielded myself completely while remaining wholly hidden, by which I mean that the emotion there is truer than anything, however true, that I say in daily speech, but it plays out in an unreal setting. The imaginary world, in which I discovered at that time so many hiding places, has never ceased to be my multiform sanctuary, my maquis and the unfailing source of my disguises. (*N. I.* 257–58)

The traditional element in Marie Noël's work is important, and was significant to her in many ways: she had roots in the soil on her father's side; for nearly 30 years she spent her summers in the countryside, and from girlhood on she was a passionate collector of traditional songs, picking them up by ear and memory from those who still knew and sang them. [Escholier, 63–66]. To bring timeless poetry out of a time-worn format is a hard mastery to acquire, and brings with it "givens" of culture and above all, language. Different cultures have their particular style and forms, developed over centuries, while the spoken languages stamp the music of their sounds and inflections on the patterns of life and the events of history. The rhyme patterns and the music of a Romance language do not transplant easily into a Germanic one, hence the fact that there are fewer of these poems in the Selection than I would wish, and as Marie Noël was past master of this style, I regret it.

In compensation, and to show that all is possible to the gifted, I slip in a poem on a girl sewing by the English poet Ruth Pitter, a near contemporary of Marie Noël, whom I feel sure she would have welcomed as a cousin [*Collected Poems*, Enitharmon Press, London, 1996, 241]:

POOR YOUNG WOMAN

Sorrow and weakness
Lie heavy on this maid;
Small earnings, great yearnings—
She loves, but is afraid;
Here she in meekness,
She in her poor attire,
Sits sewing, unknowing
The end of her desire.

But that poor rapture,
Like a thin, eager root,
Could flourish, could nourish
Some blessed leaf or shoot;
Or tower to the capture,
Like eagle in the air,
And singing, come bringing
An angel by the hair.

DIALOGUES

Marie Noël's poems are almost always a conversation of sorts: often a one-sided one, differing from a monologue only in that it implies, or at least invites, a response. She is not a poet who likes the sound of her own voice. She starts off the *Chansons* with a question: Who am I? She hasn't got the answer up her sleeve; it's a challenge issued to herself, to a potential lover, to each reader. By the end of her life, she still, I think, doesn't know, but is content to leave the question with God. In between she has spoken with, sometimes urgently interrogated—on life, on love, on death—a whole range of interlocutors, God being the principal. Scenarios are set up, put in train, but rarely, if ever, brought to a conclusion. The poem bearing the title "Dialogues" contains none: orders are barked, to which the only response is acquiescence. This is family life. The dialogue within the Trinity is much the same: in "Song of Divine Love" the Son's pleas on behalf of humankind meet with silence, family life again. In this world even the lover tries to avoid engaging. Only the poet carries on singing, in a desperate attempt to calm the storm that threatens to engulf her.

THE COMPANIONS

Another poem from the collection she thought of tenderly as the poems of her youth; yet she presents herself as already having missed life's boat. How old was she? Certainly, under thirty. It is young to give up on love, marriage, children, nor is this the only poem in this collection in which she does so: "Fantaisie à plusieurs voix" [*Oeuvres*, 68] is an astonishing five-part lament for the happiness she will never know, which ends in an attempt at resignation. The age of thirty would be thought ridiculously young today to give up all hope of marriage and children. Here in her Journal she talks about just that time in her life:

> In 1908, aged twenty-five, I was still at the awkward age, a girl who'd never blossomed.

Often ill, clumsy, unattractive with my ill-styled hair, frocks badly cut and the wretched acne which spoilt my skin. I was frightened of absolutely everyone.

But when I wasn't afraid, I was playful, mischievous and merry.

At that period the Powers that Be—Family, Church, Religion, had me under their holy thumb, they had been nursing me from infancy and hadn't yet weaned me. My heart was still swaddled in obedience and fluttering with fear.

I had already—in secret—written a lot of poems, but I was frightened of them too. There ran through them an anarchic current which upset the accepted order and seemed to me not to come from the "right place." And I kept it to myself, still stiff as a poker with morality and withdrawn into my shell like a sealed-in snail, the prisoner of my dread of the world, my mistrust of myself and the fear of God. (*N. I.* 225–26)

Les Chants de la Merci

> Whenever I can, I do things from love, as a break from the many that I do because I have to. (*N. I.* 126)

> And as rhyming wasn't all I was doing, since I was kept busy in the parish with all manner of wretchedness, I felt guilty at times to be lost in my dreams, quivering inside with hope and tenderness. So, in penitence—that is, to pull me away from this delightful self-absorption which brought comfort only to me—I started to sing the pain and misery of others as well. I made it mine. And so came to be written, at the same time as the *Chansons,* and alternating with them like virtue and caprice, the grave poems that make up the *Les Chants de la Merci*...or of the first part of that collection, the second being written a full seven years later, after a long pause caused by illness and an anxiety-ridden journey through unplumbed depths of thought. (*N. I.* 156–57)

Marie Noël had been seeking answers to her questions since she wrote her first poem, and turning outward from herself merely widened their scope. To questions thrown up by her own life, and now those of her neighbours, neither her father's philosophy nor the Church's dogma provided satisfactory answers. The battering she experienced from these not uncommon problems, together with her acute sensitivity and four years of trench warfare on her virtual doorstep brought her own interior castle down in rubble.

It was in this interval of horror, when the God of dogma failed her, that she learned the "Yes" of faith, that when truths in conflict proved irreconcilable, poetry helped her find her way to meaning. Truth, she discovered, once incarnate, was now back with the

Father beyond our fumbling grasp, and all we could touch was this outer garment.

Meaning was the path which would take her from her first poem, "Who Am I?" to the last, "Where Am I Going?" It proved a very long journey, and was not always well signposted, but at the end she saw it clear before her, and not so far away.

PART I: PRELUDE AND EXERCISES II, 2

One section of a longer poem with that title, in three main parts, it illustrates the rigorous apprenticeship of charity which she put herself through after her bargain struck with God at the age of eighteen [see above, 6]. It is my belief that, like the bargain, both poem and the passage from the Journal quoted below, reflect the constraints of family life, not her work in the community, which she would later commemorate with joyous gratitude in "Benedicat vos" [see above, 17, and below]. This poem is undated, unlike most of those in Part I of *Les Chants de la Merci,* but its placing suggests 1913–1919.

> For the love of peace…
>
> Shrink. Become less than dust, for fear that the foot of one close to you might notice and squash you.
>
> Shrink. Disappear. Out of charity. Let your words echo the words of those around you, your thoughts be as well-worn as theirs. Have no obvious existence. Push lightly aside anything that might seem to set you apart. Stay on a level with all family prejudices. Let no-one, however mediocre, feel the discomfort of suspecting in you some slight superiority…
>
> Unless it should be necessary for the salvation of this one or that.

Do what is needed, and then disappear so that all can forget.

It is very hard to *be* and be forgiven for it. (*N. I.* 60)

PART II: SONG OF DIVINE MERCY

If only Christ had created the earth!

If the Spirit of Christ had created the earth!

But Creation is not Christian, being based entirely on the necessity for each creature to destroy another.

O Christ, humbly I accept not understanding. I bow my head before the terrible darkness overshadowing the beginning. What would God be for us if He were not dark? But look and see that it is we who are the scarified field, those wounded past recovery by this divine combat between You who say: "Love!" and your Father who says "Kill!"

"Be reconciled, O Son, O Father! Until you are reconciled, what peace can I have?

Where shall we creatures find our peace, we who cannot glimpse—high as it is beyond your disaccord—the point of divine unity in the inaccessible light of your concord?

I believe in that Concord, I believe that the origin was Love. (*N. I.* 119–20)

The "Song of Divine Mercy" was one of Marie Noël's two favourite poems [*N. I.* 87], in part perhaps because it represents her first step towards the reconciliation of God with God, Creator with Redeemer. The only voice we hear is that of the Son: the mystery remains in the silence of the Father, but held safe, rather than in conflict ...for now; the fault line will remain, ever in danger of re-opening. Abbé Mugnier spends much time and effort trying to mend the breach., at best enabling her to live with it. The passage from the Journal is dated 1933–1934, shortly after the publication of the collection, and ends in a commitment to the Host, the ultimate sign of reconciliation.

On the poem's tight construction and the thought that drives it forward, Marie Noël has the following comment:

> "...In almost every word of the "Song of Divine Mercy," Evil and also mankind's submission are only just below the surface. Each line opens up a specific thought... as well as another path leading elsewhere. Take it who dares!
>
> I put into the best words I could find the meaning God entrusted to me, for whom, when or where, I have no idea. Someone will find it one day or another. Someone or no one, it doesn't matter." (Escholier, 288)

CALLING THE SHEPHERD

> The breath of God is in the prophets. But God Himself is in the mouthful of bread broken each morning by an unworthy hand.
> That is why, between a priest and seven prophets, I go to the priest.

There is one priest in this poem and, I think, two prophets. Ezekiel surely lies behind the guiding metaphor with his diatribe against the shepherds in ch. 34. I hear too an echo of Isaiah 1:4, 5, in the lines, "To the big gate bolted tight / To bar the fold," and, "He has broken down the fencing."

But only the priest is present and addressed, and he is strangely mute, as is often the case with those out of favour, including, at times, God. Marie Noël grew up in the strongly Augustinian spirituality, often referred to as Jansenist because of its rigorism, which was fostered by the parish clergy of her youth. She lost in time her childhood fear of "ces messieurs" but was left with a very moderate respect—not for the vocation, but for its representatives. In "Calling the Shepherd" she addresses to them a call, not to arms, but to suffering and service. A priest's vocation is to embrace the Sorrow of the World. The shepherd she addresses here does not seem too keen. Even at the end it is unclear whether he will respond to her urgency: his silence is perhaps the loudest in all her work.

She seems to have glimpsed at least one shepherd who met her criteria and pays him and his like a moving tribute in her journal. He is young, he looks around him and considers all the possibilities that lie open, but hears a different, compelling call:

THE COUNTRY PRIEST

"I came that I might be hated."
Bossuet, *Méditations sur l'Évangile*

> ...Oh Christ, my poor God, there you are, all alone, abandoned in your country church, with its dilapidated steeple, alone in your unswept house which no one enters, and on Sundays all you hear is the mocking sound of work on the day of rest ...
>
> So here I come! To be homeless like you; to be hated as you are; to be, like you, a shepherd without a flock, a leper cast out of the human clan, a man apart, who stands out, wears a frock, whom the villagers keep at a distance, curling a lip when he passes...
>
> ...But I'm coming, my poor Master, I'm coming to You because everyone has deserted You...I'm on my way...
>
> And the two of us, you in your distressed church, I nearby in my empty house—you, unrecognised, I held in contempt, together we'll be companions in want. (*N. I.* 39–40)

This young priest, though, sees the world as hostile rather than suffering, and it is quite possible that this slant comes from Bossuet (see quotation in the extract above, though I have not been able to trace the particular passage). Certainly poem and extract from the *Notes Intimes* both date from the 1920s. But the understanding of priesthood offered in "Calling the Shepherd" is of another order: to suffer with Christ is merely the means, not the point—the call is to love the sheep. Suffering and love can be seen as complementary, but the primacy of love is closer to the Gospel (suffering of course will follow) and also, I think, to Marie Noël's understanding of it.

Another passage in the *N. I.* better reflects her views and, interestingly, again quotes Bossuet, this time in clear disagreement. Written probably in 1933, it begins with the exclamation: "How glad I am that God is not a Saint! If a saint had created the world, he would have created the dove, but not the snake." There follows a paean of praise to the infinite diversity of God, who is artist as well as Holy One, and who would have incurred thereby the disapproval of Bossuet—whom she quotes, but again without textual reference: "Away with this perfume that damns, away with this flower...." words we will find almost unchanged in the great poem "The Greyhound," which dates from the last year of her life [see below. p. 257].

Significantly, in the poem that follows, both here and in *Les Chants de la Merci*, she tackles again the complex overlap and resolution of hatred and love.

WEEPING OVER THE MULTITUDE

A poem addressed to "la foule"—more ordinarily, a crowd, but here I think we are once more in the presence of Gospel echoes, given the suggestion of violence in the opening lines, the words "Nous vous haïssons," "we hate you," with their undertone of "Crucify him!" The poem finds its full meaning in this wider framework.

It is also a mirror image of "Exercises," where charity is seen as requiring the elimination of self in largely negative ways. Here the poet is robbed by all around her, but loses little, because what she deems precious, they don't want, and what they steal she gives before it is taken. The imagery turns this into a poem that flies, where the other plods a little.

PATHS

Who wants to find God? All paths are good for that.

For some, religion is located in feet and eyes, theirs is the charming and naïve piety of the senses. They go on pilgrimage to the great sanctuaries and bring back souvenirs—some drops of holy water, medals, rosaries. In the rue Saint-Sulpice they buy, if they are rich, fine painted statues for their parish, if they are poor, small virgins for their bedroom.

Others are moved to pious fervour by the harmonium's long-held notes, they have a penchant for tuneful hymns with seconds a third down.

These and their like feel and dream. They call Jesus their Beloved, and, as evening draws in, delight in lingering in dusk-filled churches, hands quietly folded and eyes closed.

Others, drier, less expansive, take the path of pure thought. Their prayer has no use for images. It rises straight to God, vertically, sight unseen.

Sometimes the devout consider them lacking in faith. And they in their turn can be tempted to write off the simple as foolish. Both should hold back. God is in all.

He has made ways for all, for feet—for paws even—and for wings. Ground-hugging paths with flowers and thorns,

> blackberries and wild strawberries for dear little souls, and the dizzy heights of the open sky where high fliers dare to glide in the fearful emptiness of limitless space.
>
> He has furnished a way for every hour. When great birds are weary, a branch offers a resting place, a flower quietens them, a chant restores serenity. When prayers take fright, thinking themselves lost, the light of a candle reassures them. (*N. I.* 25–26)

Marie Noël loves paths: the words "sente," sentier" "chemin," "route" chase each other through her poems. She likes the idea of going somewhere, of being on a journey. And here as elsewhere her poetry is simpler, sparer than her prose, exemplifying the truth set before us: that straight and winding paths lead ultimately to the same end. The paths in this poem are not life's tangle, they are reduced to two: the path of the learned, and that of the simple, of kings and shepherds. These are Gospel pairs, or rather, Gospel opposites, and the poet always gives the voice to the poor, to the have-nots. Here it is a man, one of a multitude on life's route march. More often it is a woman; Marie Noël was well aware of the hard and often short lives of women in her day [see "The Girl of Little Worth," and for readers happy to tackle the originals, "Sans Repos," "Le Souci," "Assomption"]. It is peculiar to the Gospel narrative that these opposites are, at the end of their different journeys, all found to be "haves," on the strict condition that the well-endowed lay their gifts at the feet of the Christ-child.

Le Rosaire des Joies

> As for *Le Rosaire des Joies*, this was my work as artist-before-God. I loved the unmixed colours, limpid and pure. Having no brush, I took up my pen and tried to paint...and I wrote, and still do, and in the same simple colours, traditional airs, lullabies and round songs. (*N. I.* 157)

The *Rosaire* was, like the *Chants de la Merci*, published in 1930, and contains, like most of her collections, poems widely spaced in time. In the *Oeuvres*, four are given the dates 1910, 1911, 1922 and, oddly, 1931. There are ten in total, if one counts the four poems grouped under the title "Visitation" as one, making it a decade of the rosary à la Marie Noël. The traditional Joys are present, and in their usual order: Annunciation, Visitation, Nativity, Presentation or Candlemas, and the Finding of Jesus in the Temple, but there is more. This is a book of stories. The poems invite reflection; like parables they lead us from the familiar into wider perspectives, yet are never abstruse. The first two titles give us five of the quietly meditative poems we might expect. But we have been alerted to "traditional airs, lullabies and round songs" and these start with the last poem of the "Visitation" quartet, the "Song of the Virgin Mary," given to alternating voices: in one couplet the Virgin describes the layette she is preparing, to which angels reply by describing the instruments of the Passion they see prophetically. Both form and content are traditional and Marie Noël herself set the words to music.

We get taken next to a Bethlehem in turmoil, stressed innkeepers, crowds arriving for the census, among them a weary couple, the young woman on a donkey, heading off to a tumbledown shelter. The poet herself slips into several poems in one disguise or another: Marie Noël has been at her dressing-up box again. The Nativity brings to the crib not shepherds, but three Old Maids offering their services to help the young mother look after her baby: they will joyfully do the skivvying. It is plain enough where those are coming from, and, as so often, irony adds a tartness to emotion, cleansing it of sentimentality. Two Mysteries and another eight poems complete the sequence. In The Finding of Jesus in the Temple, a younger "boy," who has stayed behind with him, turns back, torn between longing to keep faith with Jesus, and duty to needy parents. The family wins out, but the sense of guilt is great. Palm Sunday, and another frightened child, riding the equally nervous younger donkey of Matt. 21, follows Christ into Jerusalem. That evening the Saviour carries on to Bethany, where child and donkeys end up in the provisional peace of another stable.

The poems of the *Rosaire* were admired and cherished by both Mugnier and Bremond. Both will have understood how these Joyful Mysteries, celebrating the motherhood of Mary and the birth of the divine child, came to contain so powerful an undertow of suffering, made present in the small figure of the poet riding pillion behind the principals and holding on tight.

VISITATION

II. MAGNIFICAT

III. HOLY FAMILY

In the garden, on summer evenings, the Grown-ups who had spent all day working, after supper set about doing nothing. They would take their places on the bench outside Grandmother's door: Grandmother, Grandfather, Papa, Mamma, the tenant's children, and the maids in pink bodices doing their tatting. Above our heads the cathedral crows were leaving the tower in long lines for their woodland roosts, while

> from the neighbourhood came the sound of round-songs: the orphans were dancing in the Convent garden. (*Petit-Jour*, 43–44)

"Visitation," like "Candlemas," is a meditation on St. Luke's Gospel. It consists of a brief Prelude, followed by two poems, both situated in the house of Elisabeth and Zachary, often on its threshold, where the characters, alone or together, are shown looking out across the hilly landscape before them, usually in silence, Zachary having for the time being nothing to say, and the women, too much. Marie Noël, from the depths of her own silence, enters into their thoughts with a unique grace and discretion.

CANDLEMAS

A poem that came strangely dictated, and retained, in consequence, a special place in her heart. She describes how it began in church on the feast of Candlemas:

> That day, when the poor little February morning had barely shown its nose in the church, I had watched the candles of the procession catch light, timidly, one by one, and their tiny flames move round the choir, to return to the altar and get blown out one by one by the priest. And while reading and singing the liturgy, which tells the story of the child, its mother and father, and the two old people, I had seen, in a flash, the journey of mankind. Then that inner vision had gone out and vanished just like the candle flames ...
>
> ...Then suddenly, several weeks later, it reappeared and began to sing an incoherent song which seemed to come from outside myself, and which I took in with astonishment, word for word, as one does a dictation ...

...Next day, they were still in my head and I jotted them down on the nearest piece of paper. They formed incomplete verses, opaque, but not without charm. Someone else might have given up at that stage, but as I made out enough to render them just about intelligible without destroying their strangeness, I started to arrange them...Some verses had succeeded in doing this on their own, and where there was a gap which their inner rhythm hadn't yet joined up, I threw a little bridge across—a word or two, barely visible—to keep it going and pick it up again two or three lines further on. In this way I got to the end of the song and read it through. It was *Candlemas* as it is today. I have never been quite sure it was my own, having done nothing more than pick it up and help it to put itself in order. (*N. I.* 219–20)

Chants et Psaumes d'Automne

> Ah! I want to leave this place, to go in the fall
> Before winter comes, and fly in the wind's howl
> Where my wild heart leads and lose myself in autumn.
> My cry will pierce the desperate times and the world's
> Shroud of darkness as I make my way with the birds,
> Those that the blue of the sky has abandoned.

The lines above are from "Chant d'été," the first poem of *Les Chants de la Merci* I, written many years earlier and chosen by Marie Noël to introduce this collection of her maturity. They bridge the long interval so perfectly as to make it invisible.

> Many of my poems are true in advance, like prophecies. So that when they have grieving voices, they frighten me. (*N. I.* 135)

In the collection, *Chants et Psaumes d'Automne*, published in 1947, but written largely in the 20s and 30s, she returns from the commonality of *Les Chants de la Merci* to the personal of the original *Chansons*. The first section, the "Chants," is further subdivided, into "Chants sauvages"—once again that adjective with its multiple layers of meaning:—where, of ten poems (one included below), a number personify aspects of nature, and many are dark, some in unexpected ways. The second subsection of nine poems, of which five figure here, starting with "Dream and Song in the Snow," is headed "Chants Inquiets," "Songs of Disquiet." More personal, and among her most beautiful, they tease with meaning: she needed to write them, but did not want fools rushing in, so they are surrounded with thorn hedges.

The last section of the collection, entitled "Psalms" and written at the height of her powers, contains her darkest work; these poems are again grouped, the first under the title "Tenebrae."

I. SONGS

THE ESCORT

A village funeral, probably at Diges, no doubt very like that of Marie Noël's nurse who died in 1924.

> She was buried yesterday. All her relations from the villages round about had come to her funeral, a calm and plaintive village ceremony, bathed in the early morning peace of the fields. I recognised people and they recognised me. You who are always on the move, you have no idea how sweet it can be, to be addressed in three or four ordinary villages as "Mam'zelle Marie." (From a letter to her godfather, *N. I.* 51)

DREAM AND SONG IN THE SNOW

> "*Songe et Chant dans la Neige*—1920–26—(extracts from a sort of Christmas story, "The Angels' Christmas," too sentimental, which I dropped.)" While changing a number of lines, Marie Noël ended by publishing the essential of this poem. (Escholier, 383)

This snippet of information, vouchsafed by the poet and slipped in by her biographer might serve as a warning. In attempting to piece her truth together from the clues scattered through the forest like the trail left by Hansel and Gretel, it is all too easy to lose one's way, and one may end up at the house of the wrong witch. This is a poem best read as one of those songs that came to a girl at her spinning-wheel and is now ours to make what we want of it.

The more pious enthusiasts for her earlier work found this new collection, particularly the "Psalms" short on charm and too dark for their liking. For others it has represented the summit of her attainment.

SONG IN THE WIND

Perhaps her finest "Song of Disquiet." The wild autumn wind is an image of the poet, both are intent on protecting their child, the suffering inner self, from the vulgar curiosity of the crowd. The child, whose condition is incurable, will die if exposed to this intrusion. The wind doesn't have to explain itself, simply existing is its privilege, the poet is tempted or betrayed into half-confession. This ever-present conflict between withholding and confession is an integral part of the suffering. Hidden but visible, dying, yet surviving. Narrator and nurse and child are one.

SONG ON THE RIVER BANK

Eight of these "Songs of Disquiet" were written between 1920 and 1925, and four of them mourn the loss of a lover. These were the years of her breakdown followed by a slow recovery, itself interrupted by bouts of physical ill-health. When giving Raymond Escholier the precise dates, she adds of the poems, "They were above all imaginative, but steeped in the melancholy that possessed me at that time." [Escholier, 383] This was also a time when she suffered the break-up of a friendship which clearly mattered to her a lot, as she writes of it in some detail in her letters to Abbé Mugnier. It seems clear that this now middle-aged woman who had longed all her life to love and be loved, found it easy to slide from an intellectual friendship into an *amitié amoureuse*. Awkward exchanges of letters with the "friend," alternating with silence and months of agonising, get summed up like this: "Ah, Monsieur l'Abbé, how I tremble when I glimpse a happiness. I love it so, and it may be that this is a great disorder, a real sin. But for now, I am behaving as though it wasn't, and I am simply the great friend of my great friend. Is this a weakening? ...Or a progress?" [Mugnier, 135] The Abbé replied wisely by return: "You want to live, and you are frightened of living...There is a wide margin between living and sin" [ibid., 136]. So, yes, the poems themselves were products, like all good poems, of the imagination, but the agony was real.

Writing of the broken metre she uses in this and in "Song in the Wind," she talks of "stumbling alexandrines" in this last, and of "irregular rhythm" in "Song on the River Bank":

> These songs were like the distress of a little girl who has run away from home and got lost, but who is being held by the hand and brought home secretly by some little known but caring nurse. (*N. I.* 201)

WILL AND TESTAMENT

> Kept close in a good, faithful house in a provincial town, fenced in by duties, closely watched by the older generation, cut off from the wider world and even from my surroundings...
>
> God has been all the space I've had.
>
> In Him I found my freedom and my highroads, I braved my mountains and my precipices, like others, more than any other, I embarked on adventures and faced dangers. (*N. I.* 196)

This and the following poem both date from 1920, when she was in breakdown. She has arrived at a place where the present is unbearable and yet there is no way out. The two poems have much in common and as much again that differentiates. In the first she makes her will. This is a strong statement. A will is a hard-edged thing, as much an exercise of power as of generosity. The reverse of open-ended, it is a poor vehicle for conveying meaning. Insofar as this will is symbolic, it works like a steel safe and imprisons the poet, she finds herself bruising her elbows. Being a fine poet, she overcomes the constraints to a degree, but meaning and symbolism struggle to get free. Her inner life is painted with delicate brush strokes, somewhat at odds with the context. But who is the stranger who plays the central role in this and in the following poem? In "Will and Testament" it is never clear: a passer-by who refuses any further intimacy, yet by his (or her?) smile conveys a mysterious salvation and is rewarded equally mysteriously. A Christ-like figure—Christ being the only one on whom we can unload our sins and failings? The long final verse (a subconscious glance forward at "Jugement"?) is more opaque than open-ended.

THE FACE

> It was in these depths that the one great journey of my life took place, my descent into the abyss, my adventure, my face-to-face with danger. It was there that I had to go so that I might come back, burdened with the destiny of humankind, instead of staying for ever pure and fast asleep in my little garden with the Cross to keep me safe. (*N. I.* 105)

In "The Face" she returns to the music of the alexandrine to look at her life from another angle, and the change of rhythm proves wonderfully liberating. The poetry is singing once more, we are in a parallel world where nothing is fixed and which makes its own meaning. This is an overview of a life half lived, yet the end is already apparent, for time is collapsed into itself. On different levels and from yet further angles, the journey into the abyss and back will be recounted again in the four first poems of *Psalms*, but it is in "The Face," as befits one of her *Chansons*, that the emotional level is at its zenith.

Here we find again the passer-by who enables the poet to struggle on, not this time by smiling, but with a look of pity. But here the "chanson" format renders the unknown familiar. Surely this is Christ, in the form, perhaps, of a Samaritan, stepping out of the heart of the storm to save the wounded traveller? And at whom, other than Christ, is she going to look up, on the threshold of eternal life, with the face lit by the pity shown to her in her abasement?

I would also like to draw attention to one line in this poem and discuss it briefly in its original French, because it expresses in condensed form a significant theme in her life and poetry and will reappear in almost identical words in two other poems, of which the second, on her approaching death, is possibly the last she wrote. These clues are essential to its understanding.

Here, in "The Face," the fifth verse begins: "But summon rather from among my guises / The down-and-out girl in the tattered dress"—in the original, "Celle d'une pauvresse en robe déchirée."

The word "pauvresse" designates a pauper, a term no longer current in English, but the sense is important, and she will use it again. As for the verb "déchirer," to rend or tear, it will reappear in each of these three poems, identifying her as "the girl in the torn dress," it is *who* she is, her badge of suffering. Each time we find it, it will carry this weight.

II. PSALMS: TENEBRAE

> On the evening of All Saints, at 6 o'clock, my grandmother and I would disappear into the great Night of the Cathedral, which at that hour, under the stupendous vaulting, had neither beginning nor end.
>
> In the tower the passing bells were tolling...those admirable passing bells of the Cathedral of Auxerre, a tragic group of deep-voiced bells that would burst out suddenly sobbing—five or six notes that rent the air—before falling back again into a silence from which, after an anguished pause, they would re-emerge, lifting their voices in disconsolate tears drawn from who knows what wells of pain and fear. (*N. I.* 307)

Tenebrae—darkness or shadows, is the word used to designate the morning office of the last days of Holy Week. It also the subtitle she gives in French to this subsection of six "Psalms," of which the first four follow in translation. These are the Psalms she sang during her Passiontide at Bellevue, her time in the abyss. The sixth, the "Psalm of the Foolish Virgin" is not included here.

DESTINY

> My youth was dying little by little in loneliness; and lonely as I was, on the corner of an ordinary path, just like the others, behind my thirty or forty years of banal virtue someone was waiting, biding his moment, and pounced to punish me. I never had been punished until then, I was just a little girl...
>
> ... And he, the Unknown, had laid a trap for me. He had waited a long time, in silence, for the moment of exhaustion, to tip me into a horror of myself and hand me over to the combined demons of body and soul. (*N. I.* 104)

These lines in her Journal date from 1934–1935. The quintet of poems which recount this episode were probably newly written, as she ends the long passage from which the extract is taken with the words:

> Until now, I have been afraid to go and look at myself in the well into which I had fallen...afraid to tell, or even whisper, this story, as I was asked to do. But the calm of evening has fallen. I have been able to look back. It is done.
>
> And now, Lord, let us not speak of it again.

Destiny, the introduction, is a mixture of innocent light-heartedness and menace, the latter hidden in the scriptural allusions. The child narrator is alone, telling her story; when it goes wrong there is no one else to blame, but can a child be blamed?

ILL-MET

> But what can I do?
>
> In the yawning depths I foundered in last year I had a glimpse of God that I cannot now forget...God!...but not the God I had known so well since childhood, the familiar God, "Our Father," ...my Friend...No! Another!
>
> Another, hidden behind Him and so terrible that my reason was shaken. The God who wrote only one Law on his silent Tablets: "You shall kill...you shall be killed," and who never bothered with any explanation other than the implacable course of the Universe. Why would He? He rules us more surely through what is unfathomable in our instincts, than God the Word does through his revelations and with the consent of our mind. (*N. I.* 22)

Gone is the deceptive light-heartedness of "Destiny': there is menace present from the outset. And who are the unspecified "they" (in French the still vaguer "on') who are now in charge? "They," it transpires, are her natural guardians, the grown-ups, the family; for she is still a child, in experience and understanding, if not in age. And they have used Truth itself, the Cross of Christ, to keep truths hidden behind a barricade of rules and practice. Having done their duty, they don't much like the result, and send her off to finish her education in the wild wood, place of misadventure, warning her to avoid above all things meeting her own soul. Having no idea what that is, inevitably she comes across it, in the form of a stagnant pool, and falls straight in: it is indeed her destiny.

In "Destiny," she was truly fated, but also fond of her own way. In "Ill-Met" she doesn't even know what her own will is. And where "Faces" is a poem about suffering, "Ill-Met" is about sin and evil: the first moves us, the second can frighten, it calls up the hideous nightmares of children, to which Marie Noël had been subject. While all adults have seen naked suffering, few have seen evil naked. Memory dredges up childhood terrors in these and other poems: a corner of her grandparents' garden, that Eden of loaded fruit trees, well-drilled vegetables and rambling roses, hid a small greenish pond half-hidden by ivy, with a sinister air which put her off looking into its depths; and when she was five or so, the sickening climbs up long stepladders in water mills, afforded a view between little feet of the gurgling river below [*Petit-Jour,* 112, 117]. The pond has figured already in another poem, its water "old and deceptively sweet, full of turgid sin" ["Prière d'avant la vie," *Oeuvres,* 403].

As the poet comes back shaking from what she has seen, she meets "the good believers / Passing by, men, women, all," who don't seem too pleased to see her return. Among them are perhaps those who encouraged her to go. "Let us close the staring eyes / Of the pit with long straws," suggest helpfully her fellow Christians, and "throw some wood, criss-cross / dead sticks ...So that, too scared to look / At the yawning hole down there, / Dusk looming, the benighted girl / Will step on it, hands in prayer."

SONG OF THE GUARDIAN

> It was a great battle: the hour of the Power of Darkness—months of hell, months of suffering, the dying of many deaths...
>
> I came back step by step, down a long, long path, rough but dead straight: obedience. Less a path than a barely visible rope you cling to in the bottom of the pit. I never let go. I knew nothing, I said nothing, I submitted, I obeyed:
>
> "Don't open your eyes...ever. Say "yes" to God, come what may. Do as you are told. Cross the pit on a straw ...The only safety lies in walking blind." (*N. I.* 104–105)

This is the message of the companion poem to "Ill-Met," "Song of the Guardian," in which Marie Noël chronicles her hard way back through grace to understanding. They form a remarkable pair, the short six and seven syllable lines of the first evoking the urgency of many of her poems in traditional form. In the second, less visual, more meditative, she returns to the classic alexandrine, not the irregular eleven syllable line she made her own in the more plaintive "Songs." And yes, the way is hard, but once she has made it back to *terra firma*, she is allowed to become for a time a little girl again, while her angel cares for her with maternal solicitude, to the point of washing her soiled dress—the baptismal robe?

Destiny/Fate has its place in this poem too: there is no escaping its "baiser déchirant"—laceration is part of the human experience.

STORM

One might have thought that three poems on the subject had done it justice, but the longest, and in some ways the most powerful was in reserve. It flies higher, farther, is more encompassing: there is nothing there but this great wind blowing, and yet, by the end she has explored the problem of evil, how it came to be, wondered why God does nothing about it, and at the end, as usual, has received no answer: she carries on singing, to save her soul.

Picking the poem up five years later to rework it in her summer retreat at Diges—not without trepidation—she writes, as ever when insecure, to Abbé Mugnier.

> I have taken up again, because of the fine and violent rhythm of a great storm, a poem which I might not have dared to dig down into if you weren't around to give me courage in your very silence. It is the poem of my "Darkness" ...that I lived through before I wrote it—the song of the abyss into which I fell ...from which I climbed back out and am leaving ever farther behind as I walk at last in that anticipation of eternal rest offered by the peace of the last years of our life when the mind has got used to the half-light—a state that God kindly grants us—instead of crying in the night like a trapped animal ...Pray for me specially just now, that I may get to the end of my dark Song without breaking my wings. (Diges, 15:7:39, Mugnier, 337–38)

In fact, two months later she would be in a country at war, and the following years would test her to the limit, without ever again putting her emotional or spiritual stability in danger. Her view of herself sinking into the tranquil half-light of old age has a comical element, for us who have hindsight.

The medieval octosyllable employed in three of these poems, gave Marie Noël a freedom she revelled in. Perfect for the traditional song, she used it also as a way to push open the door to the wide world. It could be moving, serious or playful in her hands. Here, in this great quartet, the first two poems are in octosyllabic quatrains, the fourth in verses of alternating eight- and three-syllabic lines, where each first and third line falls inevitably into the following—that "dying fall." Yet how differently she can use these metres. The first poem, "Destiny," trips along with the gaiety of a little girl going out for a walk, which is indeed the subject, until readers start tripping in turn on the scriptural underpinnings marked: Beware, beware!—and may thus avoid falling into the stagnant pond.

The second poem, "Ill-Met" doesn't catch us out in the same way: it is darker from the start and we are more prepared. It goes on to prove just how sinister in different hands this metre, dear to the Goliards for their drinking songs, can be.

The last poem of the four, "Storm," pushes the form to a new extreme. Of some verses we are tempted to ask: How much theology can she pack into the same number of syllables as two alexandrines, and the answer is: as about as much as St. Paul spreads across a letter to the Corinthians.

> After *Darkness* I will sing *Lauds* because the black talons of the mystery have loosened their clutch for a instant, letting my heart fly heavenwards like a little bird that has just had a narrow escape. (*N. I.* 106)

She did indeed add a final section in the form of a short poem entitled "Dawn," in which she takes her child at daybreak in her arms and knocks at the door of the Virgin Mary, who, of course, opens to her. The little one's eyes, she goes on to explain, have hurt so dreadfully all night long from the horrors she has looked on that she feared the child was dying. She hands her over to the Virgin to be nursed and carried gently round her garden "with little steps." The poem brings not a miracle but a ray of hope—the "little escape" or open-ended closure that most of us live with most of the time.

With regret I have not included it, as, to reproduce the formal pattern of the verse I should need to find six fitting rhymes for "Mary," the translator's equivalent of a miracle.

OFFICE FOR A DEAD CHILD

I. FUNERAL TRAIN
II.
III.
IV. CREDO
V. PRAYER
VI. DEO GRATIAS

> Shall I be consoled or punished one day for my outbursts of anger against Death? In despite of all I've read, heard, known, thought and believed in its favour, Death has always found me screaming in the face of Heaven. With me, it has always been the wild beast that has had the first say. It was only later, afterwards, that my soul would come home, and I'd bandage as best I could, with my own thoughts, the hideous, irreparable wound that Death had inflicted on one dear to me, and, far worse than that, the hurt done in me, in spite of me, to God. (*Petit-Jour*, 105)

Marie Noël lived at a time when the death of children was frequent, particularly among the poor, but there was no family not at risk. This six-part protestation against this scourge was her response to the death of her little niece in 1930 from pneumonia. Marie Noël, her godmother, was present and wrote on the subject a desperate letter to Abbé Mugnier [Mugnier, 207], as well as a passage which figures in her Journal, [*N. I.* 69–70]. The lines quoted above are taken from her own childhood memoir, while the word *hurler*, to scream, or howl, that she uses in it, echoes the title—*Hurlement*—given to a poem written after her brother Eugène's death, representing her mother's suffering and revolt.

Death in all its aspects is a recurrent throbbing pain in her correspondence with the Abbé, who deals with it patiently while accepting it as an integral part of her spirituality of suffering.

> Perhaps my religious anguish is the bittersweet grace which preserves my faith. With my kind of reasoning, I might have settled comfortably into the serene doubt of my father and many like him. Instead, I suffer. And this is my genuine way of believing. (*N. I.* 58)

Indeed, I think suffering was her *only* way of believing. She took her revolt against death and violence of any kind right back to the vegetarian Eden first created, where an unfallen humanity would still have had to take a knife to the cabbage, and pull complaining carrots from the soil (it is possible to admire the answer she finally comes up with in "Adam and Eve" without being wholly convinced by it). The child who saw a hen killed in her mother's kitchen was still fingering the scar half a lifetime later, and by the time she sat watching her three-year-old niece die of pneumonia she had seen far too much of death close-up, in war as well as peace.

The *Office pour l'Enfant Mort* is an imagined narrative, based on experience and given a setting which renders it universal, increasing the poignancy.

At the centre are the death of the child and the suffering of the mother, but death involves the whole community: the family to accompany the child to the church; the townspeople, the verger, the priest, the choirboys, the sexton, the friends and neighbours, all with specific roles. The mother then finds herself alone at the grave with her memories of her child's last hours, and of the small kindnesses of women on their knees round the cot, doing what Marie Noël herself had so often done, praying the rosary, fetching and soothing... Finally, God is called to account. The father of the child is never mentioned.

The first three despairing chants are in octosyllabic couplets, hard, terse and to the point. As the mother dissolves into her grief the form grows more complex, time slows down. Part VI, headed *Deo Gratias*, stands slightly apart, and is sometimes printed as an individual poem. The form, again, is different. It is as though it belongs without belonging: the Psalm is sung by a community of nuns, praying in their enclosure for those outside it. Their chant carries the suffering of the world up to heaven, where it falls, broken with its weight of tears, on the feet of the Almighty... Thanks be to God.

The last word may be left to the poet:

> I read my "Office for a Dead Child" to Abbé Mugnier.
>
> While I was writing it and it was holding me completely captive, I was seized with fear and didn't dare finish it. A priest reassured me: "Get it out of your system; decisions can come later."
>
> For Abbé Mugnier it was saved by the crowning lines:
>
> But if it's You, what can I say?
> Bad is good and yea is nay...
>
> where the violence of the revolt dies on the shore, its roar sinking into an act of faith.
>
> But I find it upsetting to read aloud and it's my hope that

> one day it may be allowed to lie in a book, silent, like a mad woman whose shrieking scares the neighbours. (*N.* I. 71)

EVENING HYMN

Links between Journal and poetry may span years. "Evening Hymn" is placed between the "Office for a Dead Child" and the great poem "Judgment" which we know was finished in 1938, and is presumably of the same period. Undisguisedly personal, it examines her life up to that point, each stanza baring a nerve of suffering, and each in the last line finding in that suffering an equivalent saving grace. She writes as of a truth just seized upon. Twenty years later, probably in 1958, this comforting truth resurfaces as she looks back, serene:

> On turning round today to look back at the past, I see that all through my years of sorrow, of darkness suffered in patience, of daily wretchedness, when I was embarrassed by my faults, hampered by my failings, thwarted by countless hindrances, I was travelling by the divine road, carried, O God, like an invalid, the whole way in your arms. (*N. I.* 326)

With Marie Noël it is almost always the immediacy of the struggle to wring understanding out of pain which produces the poetry, not the looking back with Wordsworth at the daffodils.

In "Evening Hymn" there is a backward glance to "Will and Testament" and the mysterious stranger's smile which is invoked again here in verse 5. The smile of this unknown "neighbour" compensates generously for the many wounds inflicted by those closer to home. This seeking for the point of balance in the working of Providence was important to Marie Noël.

Chants d'arrière-saison

For Escholier, *Chants et Psaumes d'Automne* was without a doubt Marie Noël's greatest collection, the pinnacle of her inspiration, and few would disagree with him. That wild autumn wind would never blow again in the same way. Autumn had set in early with Marie Noël, the poems were all written between the ages of 37 and 50; but her spring had been prolonged and summer got squeezed to death by a bad angel. Her "autumn" years were those when she came into the fullness of her creative powers. What followed was perhaps a decrease in energy rather than a diminution of what we like to call inspiration. Above all she was on a more level plane, the storm was over, the tree was no longer being shaken to its roots.

As a collection *Chants d'Arrière-Saison* lacks a unifying principle, there is no "major work." She has gathered, in half a dozen subsections with evocative titles, the poems written since 1940, along with earlier ones still uncollected, and sent them to the publisher. Only the historical are dated. Of some forty poems, if none perhaps merits the term "great," a large number are undoubtedly excellent, a few may get ticked as favourites, all are worth their place in a fine poet's Works. I have not retained the subdivisions, the result would have been too bitty.

Abbé Mugnier was to die in March 1944, in his own bed in Paris. His protégée had read him her undeniably great "Jugement" six years earlier and received his blessing. The war prevented further meetings, but their letters continued. His leaving, however sad, was for her as providential as his coming over twenty years before: he had seen her through it all, even the Occupation: she would miss him, but she would manage. He died old and blind and at peace; she would follow in his steps, but there was still a long way to go, and the *Chants d'Arrière-Saison* was just another milestone on the road.

THE ROAD OF NOT TODAY

The title of this poem that opens the collection, "Le Chemin du Refus," is a translator's nightmare multiplied by five, this being the number of times it figures, like a refrain, in the verses. There is nothing that closes a door as sharply as that tight "u" at the end of "refus," which English speakers can only imagine because they have problems in pursing their lips enough to pronounce it. "Refyoosle" will not do. It was looking back up the byways of history that gave me an alternative. Tradesmen and pedlars, on foot, later in vans, cried their wares round the back streets of towns and down country lanes, and the women who answered the knock or were caught outside, would sing out, "Not Today!" I have lent the expression to Marie Noël. It is not as cutting as hers, but taking the form of direct speech, might be said, to open up one more perspective: the naysayer gains a voice but is seen to be also a loser. Come journey's end, the poet will have learnt that the hurts don't matter, that *all* are in fact wounded and all need forgiving ["Swan Song"].

This is one of those octosyllabic poems she has made her own: intensely personal and yet universal, made so here by the introduction of Christ, seen by her but heard by none, as poor as herself yet addressed as Lord. It bridges the whole mystery from Incarnation to Ascension in everyday dress and common language.

CLOSURE

> "The field that got lost at the end of my childhood"—
>
> Once, just before the onset of evening, [my nurse] took me

> far away, to the end of the world, where in a mysterious field we cut tall-growing ferns with a sickle. I have never found this field since. But there was a happiness there at the edge of the sunlight which was on the point of withdrawing. How did we arrive there together without road or path? (*N. I.* 51)

This field, with its fleeting happiness, haunted her for most of her life, if one can be haunted by yearning as well as by fear. It became not quite otherworldly, but almost: heaven's antechamber. It creeps into her Journal two or three times, once in verse, and is flowered with detail in *Petit-Jour* [139–41]. She goes looking for it, but never quite finds it and ends up saying sadly: "It was 1891, I was eight years old." [*N. I.* 292] Then in 1965, just two years before her death, she has to call an electrician to her house in Auxerre for a minor repair. As they chat, he tells her that he has read *Petit-Jour*, "and I know that road you can't find, I know where it runs." And he describes it then and there, for her, for all of us:

> Ah! Yes, it is, it is! That very one, my lost road lying between those high banks of chalk from which one can see the valley… (*Marie Noël et Auxerre*, 63–65)

She has made quite sure that it won't be forgotten.

OLD WOMAN

> I have looked for somewhere to live. I've walked for a long time, I'm old, and I still haven't found it.
>
> I am looking for somewhere to die.
>
> There must be bright sunshine, to warm my heart as I fall asleep, and the earth there must be soft and secret, to take me and cover and hide me. (*N. I.* 24)

THE LAST GRIEF

A poem that only she could have written. Who else has personified aspects of their emotional life and let them occupy the fireside stool? Medieval writers, with whom she was familiar, allegorised, but formally and on the grand scale. This is a tragic Wonderland that Lear and Carroll would have recognised instantly and been at home in. Elsewhere she acknowledges an affection for the most faithful of her griefs—the one that never leaves her, snuggling up to her even in bed—and pleads with reluctant angels to allow her into heaven:

> So big is she, she's very small / And never says a word / And if she sometimes cries a bit / It's without being heard. ["Chant de la Peine," *Oeuvres*, 555].

VIATICUM

Although the recoil from physical corruption is still there, a dawning acceptance of death can be seen in the last verse. The only anger in the poem is directed against the well-intentioned who would intervene, the poet wants the one thing that matters, the laissez-passer to salvation. It is not a peaceful poem, but there is a chink of light down the edge of that heavy door.

THE SPRING

> ...the continual surrender of self for the love of Christ to what in others was so "other," so alien. (*N.* I. 222)

> Love: a spring that thirsts. (*N. I.* 311)

A BITTER LEAVE-TAKING

When I come to die, I shall ask forgiveness of this one or that for not having loved them enough, and, even more, of another, for having loved to excess.

To love to excess: a lack in love.

To love to excess: an injustice. That inflicted by hunger on the prey.

To love too much is not to love *one another* too much. In mutual love, there is no limit. Each one fills and absorbs the other.

But for one who loves little or not at all, to be loved to excess is a heavy burden to bear.

Loving, what is left to do when all has been done and lost.
(*Marie Noël et Auxerre*, Zodiaque, 1992, 35–36)

SONG OF THE ROBE

This is the second poem in which we meet the "robe déchirée," the torn dress, or robe. Here its meaning is extended by scriptural allusions. It is the Robe of Love worn by the King; it is also the seamless garment for which the soldiers drew lots, the garment which Christ wore while carrying his Cross. It is his Robe of Suffering, which he shares with the poet, for whom it is "his and mine." But she at that stage sees it only as the robe of comfort: it will protect her, keep her safe and warm, and one day will become the robe of glory. So the King, without explanation, takes it back, rips it and returns it, no longer windproof. Complaint brings the wherewithal to mend it and hours—years?—are spent darning and patching, all to no avail:

the winter wind, with its icy breath, finds its way through and into her very heart by way of "la grande déchirure," the great laceration of death.

This is the key poem which takes us from "Faces" to those written in the last year of her life: "Swan Song" and "The Greyhound." All her life Marie Noël wrestled with the silence with which God met her every question—about death, about the origin of evil, about the inherent clash between nature and nurture, eating and nourishing.

Whether she ever resolved this paradox in which the God of Love finds himself apparently boxed, is for others to say—or not. I suspect it unravelled in her heart rather than her head. It is to her last poems and the last pages in her Journal that we must turn, not for answers, but for pointers.

MARTHA AND MARY

The duality of the Gospel sisters was lived out by Marie Noël in so literal a way, yet their names are rarely evoked in her Journal. In the letters to the Abbé Mugnier, Martha comes into her own, serving as shorthand for "not a moment for poetry." In December 1923 she tells the Abbé that she must find a refuge somewhere, as she was turning into "Mary in distress" since her mother's dependence on her at every moment had deprived her of "the better part". Ten years later her health, at least, is better. But the demands on her have, if anything, increased:

> Oh, to be myself!
>
> I'm lost in the lives of others.
>
> If only I could be me again, untamed as I was in my youth when nobody noticed or took account of me, when I didn't matter to anyone, but was just my own song...

> ... "Mary, Mary, why do you bother with all these things which aren't your business?"—"It's because Martha has left me to do all the serving on my own. Shall I complain then? No! I've been happy to serve. But how I'd have loved still to be me, me and my thoughts, my song, my prayer, the me I liked best and am so happy being, in secret, now and then. (*N. I.* 133)

It must have been then or thereabouts that she wrote this poem. Certainly, as a poet she had the double gift of rendering the specific universal, and of presenting a general situation as hers or yours or mine, but here it is surely hers: from the mid-thirties onward she had two old women to look after, a bedridden aunt with dementia, and her mother, with all her wits, but increasingly exacting—so we have ill-tempered Martha relaxing on her pillows, while Mary scurries round as an unappreciated skivvy with no time left for contemplation.

OUT AND ABOUT

Behind this poem lies history in the form of a narrative written and sent in 1947 to Escholier, which allows us to look over a poet's shoulder. In the poem the story has been boiled down into a few factual details and these in turn rendered into an essence of meaning. The memories will vanish like the people present; the meaning will live on, to be quickened in fresh minds. The letter to Escholier includes Marie Noël's tart comment on her mother's behaviour: "Madame Rouget is beginning to realise that the day that marks her daughter's emancipation is definitely out of the ordinary"—out of the ordinary too that it took that daughter fifty-seven years to emancipate herself.

In "Out and About," one of the white-haired women is myself. Do your best to imagine your trembling cousin as lady-commandant among a crowd of bewildered people in a cellar... My neighbour Lucie Rouxel and I had been kept busy looking for help—unsuccessfully—and organising the rescue of a paralysed man abandoned in a house in the bombed quarter. Which is why, instead of staying in the cellar like well-brought up girls who never leave Mother, we had been "out and about," with the planes overhead no longer dropping bombs, but passing the time sporadically machine-gunning this and that.

Back in the cellar by four o'clock, we heard motor cycles going down the street past our door. Scouts. The German army was coming this way, not the army of occupation which was taking the Paris road, but the fighting forces making post-haste for Gien-[sur-Loire] ...We could already hear the rumble of tanks in the distance, and, closer, the sound of machine guns rattling away at anything suspect.

Remembering at that point the strategic instructions applicable to our situation, given me at some point by some officer or other, I ordered my company—yes, cousin, I did!—to evacuate the cellar at once to avoid us being "mopped up," which wouldn't have been at all amusing.

My troops were obeying orders when I came up against an unforeseen obstacle: Mother! Mother in a furious temper! The poor thing had been there all day with two trusted carers. When I took her arm to lead her out, first come, first saved, she gave me a fierce shove. "Oh, so Someone's remembered I exist! It wasn't like that earlier, Someone had better things to do. Now I see I'm to be fetched, but it's too late, now! Just leave me be! I'm going nowhere!"

Now it's the turn of the rest who won't leave until she has, and who stand waiting for her to simmer down and to forgive me! In vain I plead with her. The rumbling grows louder. "You'll get us all killed!" I shout. "Too bad!" comes the heroic retort.

At that, cousin, I swap the scolded schoolgirl expression for the voice of authority and give the order to evacuate the cellar...And then comes the army. Tanks, artillery, motorised divisions started to roll in around 4.30 on Saturday, June 15th, and carried on until the evening of Tuesday 18th, without pause or intermission, all thundering through at 50 mph....

"I've always wanted to tell you the story of that day. Here it is together with 'Out and About.'" (Escholier, 342–43)

KEEPING VIGIL

Here, each evening, there comes a splendid moment: the homecoming of the oxen with the great cartload of sheaves towering over them. Led by a taciturn German P.O.W., stripped to the waist, who walks at their head with a rhythmic tread, and touches them with the goad without even turning his head, they appear, slow and majestic, to come straight out of eternity.

Maybe Boaz saw their like.

And maybe that is the true rhythm of work, the one God devised for man, that noble gait, that powerful, unhasting tread.

Perhaps our Cathedrals were conceived and built without hurry or fret, and with the steady calm of mind and hands and only the vigorous effort measured to the day's need.

Perhaps all human labour, be it of soul or body, requires for its beauty something of the grandeur of time. (Hauterive, August 1946, *N. I.* 276)

Marie Noël's calendar stretched from Eden to the Apocalypse with staging posts between. "Keeping Vigil" was written in 1947, when the longed-for peace was not so peaceful after all. Hiroshima and Nagasaki were still atomic bomb sites, India and Pakistan were preparing for war, the Soviet Union was taking control of governments in Eastern Europe, and the Prime Minister of France mobilised troops against striking miners. This poem forms part of a subsection entitled "*Chants des Temps en Feu*," comprising two poems on World War I, three on World War II, and two best described as "apocalyptic," the second, dated 1960, undisguisedly so.

THE LAST MASS: OFFERTORY

"Offertory" is the first part of "The Last Mass," the poem which closes the *Chants d'Arrière-Saison*. In the second and longer part, "Benedicat Vos," the blessing, she remembers at length and in detail those to whom she owes her existence, starting with her forebears and continuing with the many who have touched her life and made it what it is. It is a thoughtful and generous tribute to all who have both helped and hurt her.

In "Offertory" her embrace is wider, taking in not only humankind but the whole of creation, each part and element serving another, dying that something else may grow. There is nothing created which this interdependence doesn't extend to, and all comes together in the bread of suffering and the wine of love offered here on the altar. It is summed up in the term Ember Days: days of fasting and abstinence which disappeared from the calendar with the liturgical changes adopted after Vatican II; few will now remember them. They introduced the four seasons of the year, recalling the seesaw of famine and glut, scrimping and greed, winter cold and summer drought, labour of seedtime and joys of harvest.

Written probably around 1960, the poem forms a sharp contrast in tone and style with the passage below written on New Year's Eve, 1940. The fierce, unforgiving irony of the prose piece strikes a note that clashes with the verses where line slips singing into smoothly crafted line. Yet both pieces are driven and animated by pity—pity for the inhabitants of Diges and Usy and the back streets of Auxerre, broadening out like floodwater to irrigate the uncharted deserts of the world.

TE DEUM, 31 December 1940

On the last day of the year, the Good Lord was in Heaven and looking down on a church where the people were engaged in singing him the *Te Deum*. The church had no longer bell-tower or bells, and the parish priest had done his best to block up the biggest holes in walls and roof, keeping the faithful more or less dry on rainy days while they said their prayers.

Present today was Léontine, whose three houses had been burnt down and who was lodged now in a cold attic. Present was Thérèse, to whom the Germans had left neither furniture nor clothes and who had come to office in her neighbour's coat. There was François from les Noues, all of whose horses and cows had been taken by the troops, so he could no longer plough his acres, and beside him on the bench sat poor Madeleine, whose husband had been shot on the village outskirts. Lame Germaine was there, whose three sons were prisoners...As was Théodore, whose wife and two daughters had died together, crushed when the barn fell... And Marguerite, who had lost her little boy as they fled, and nobody knew what had become of him...and Vincent whose old mother had burnt to death in the car...And Jean-Pierre who had lost both eyes in a shell-burst...and all the rest who don't know where to turn or what to eat, as the enemies were emptying fields, stables and shops of all remaining food. There were a lot of them there, all together, sitting close, filling the church. Some were in tears. But all were singing in careful, pious voices the *Te Deum* of the last day of the year—for all the graces and favours received in the course of the year—just as their old priest had told them to.

The good Lord, listening to them, was bowled over with admiration, and said to the Angels:

"In truth, mankind is a holy creation. Look at these poor people: twelve months ago they entrusted their year to me to ensure that it came safely to harbour, and I loaded it for them with calamities and horrors; they prayed each day to be delivered from evil, and I delivered them up to the worst; they pleaded for peace, and I loosed on them the dogs of war; they asked for daily bread, and I have kneaded for them a hunger that will leave many of them dead; they thought they were placing their families and their homeland in safety in my hands, and I crushed the second and broke up the first ...Certainly I had my reasons ...I cannot hold back from letting the weight of a country's faults collapse on it; I cannot clean a dirty world without turning it upside down, as I did in the days of Noah, when I had to do a thorough sluicing. But that is my work as God which none but me can make sense of. Mankind doesn't know what I am doing, nor towards what good end I am working, they just put up with it. And yet listen to them praising and thanking me as though I had preserved their poor little lives in accordance with their poor little prayers. Truly, their faith is great, and they love me with a wonderful love. O my children, my children! ...Listen to them singing *Sanctus! Sanctus!* at the top of their voices. You too, Angels, Prophets and all you Saints, sing in Heaven a hymn in honour of these whose ill-fortune renders me glory."

With that our Good Lord intoned: *Te hominem laudamus*—and the Angels took up the chant and praised humankind.

God, O God! disappointment without end.
You whom we think and do not know ...
Whom we love with all our strength and will never embrace ...
Who eternally draw us and ever escape...
God, O my God whom I have sought so intensely, where are you this evening? (*N. I.* 241–43)

Chants des Quatre-Temps

> Loving with a heart swept clean
> Of the lees of love deceived:
> Thus my soul—God take it home
> To the country which is his. (*Ch. des Q-T*, 7)

This is Marie Noël's last collection, the poems chosen and put together by herself, the late ones punctiliously dated, proving that she was still engaged in it in the months, perhaps weeks, before her death. It was her legacy, and she knew it. We know it too, by the little quatrains inserted here and there on blank pages, by the subtitle to the final section: "Footpaths through the Last Years." The title given to the book, *Chants des Quatre-Temps*, bridges the break between the last collection and the new. She has plucked the term Ember Days from "The Last Mass" and uses it to sum up a life of much fasting, some feasting, hard labour, some resting, and the coming dark lit by a candle no gale will blow out. Around half of the poems were written in the 1960s, a number are highly original: this is not the work of an old woman of failing powers. The stamina may be missing, but she is exploring new paths. These poems are astonishingly varied, some of them daringly condensed. At the same time, she was still writing the traditional songs of her twenties: three lovely and accomplished examples are dated 1964, 1966 and 1967—it is remarkable. The full alexandrine for "The Greyhound," the broken 11 syllable metre for "Swan Song," with its disquietude, a lot of the octosyllables she uses to render the shifting moods of life, all her skills with form and rhythm are on view here. A lot of shorter poems—she is getting ever more succinct as time contracts before her.

She has one or two scores still to settle, not any longer with

God, but with the Adversary, his and ours. There is a subsection, slim but significant, entitled "The Passage of the Devil," consisting of three poems, introduced by these words:

In the beginning
Love is confronted by Pride
Me!
Me, confronting the other
Love says Yes!
Pride says No!
Non serviam.

He has turned away from the Lord.
He will live in the parched places of the desert,
In the salt land, uninhabited. (Jer. 17:6)

The first poem looks at the Devil in Scripture and tradition—not his origin, that was done in "Storm"—his person and role. The poet sees him in terms of drought, the salt land of Jeremiah. He can neither bleed nor weep, the saving graces accorded to sinners.

"He, the Other, like a wall reared up
With which God's power collides.
He, the Other, without peer, the Pure,
The Unimpaired, the hard-eyed angel
PRIDE!
But LYING is worse still."

There follow two poems under the title "Gargoyles for a Cathedral," where we meet the devil as basilisk, the liar incarnate and father of lies [Jn 8:44], the serpent whose eye deals death. The second, "The Deserter," is included in this selection, and a brief commentary will be found on p. 251.

Written in 1963–1964, these poems had significance for Marie Noël. Together with the thirteen that follow, written as late or later, they contain the burden of her thoughts and prayers, her fears and aspirations, as she came to terms with the imminence of her own death. That she believed lying to be worse than pride acquires in this context a singular weight; curious too that the woman born in the Maison du Diable, should reserve a place for him in this last of her lodgings.

THE DUMB GIRL'S SONG

The poem which opens her last collection, a choice she will have given thought to, is undated, as are all of the first seven poems bar one, which bears the date 1929; another, "A Bird," we know to have been written in 1928 [see below, p. 248]. The content, though, speaks for itself. If the theme—a girl's love-life wrecked by parents—is traditional, the rendering is exceptionally bitter. While using a theme does not imply self-identification, it seems indisputable that the beating heart of this poem is the dismissal in 1904 of a tentative lover by her mother, presumably with her father's knowledge and approval. Forty years is a long interval, but a number of indications suggest that "The Dumb Girl" was written in the aftermath of her mother's death in 1941. It was 1944 that saw the publication of *Le Chemin d'Anna Bargeton,* which recounts this unfortunate story, giving it a different outcome. The deaths of those closest to us are liable to spark off strong and sometimes conflicting emotions, and because this is a poem, the dumb girl can act out the revenge the poet would never have taken. Poets like actors can play many roles, and have the advantage of writing their own scripts.

Escholier, who did not know the poem, probably kept in a drawer like many others, clinches the matter by quoting this extract from her unpublished juvenilia of 1903–1905, the "Songs of Cinderella":

> My arms are folded on my heart
> To keep my melancholy hid
> Where none can see.
>
> ...My hand is pressed across my mouth
> To stop my cry of fierce revolt
> From coming out...
>
> ...It is a right claimed by the old
> To take away from lass and lad
> Head-turning hope.
>
> Father, sleep on, and mother too,
> Love was shown the door by you,
> I bow my head.

He reads these verses as a reference to the story that he had heard originally from Mme Rouget and recognised in *Anna Bargeton.* The echoes in "Song of the Dumb Girl," still clearer in the original French, are undeniable.

I DO NOT KNOW

> I was so small and had such modest tastes that I would never have dreamt of Paradise and Bliss if I had only been able to settle down quietly in a warm corner of the earth, in my own little house, turned to catch the summer sun, and filled in winter, behind the window panes, with light and warmth and beloved presence.

With that very modest happiness, providing it had lasted, I wouldn't have needed Heaven.

But God had greater ideas for me than I did. He hasn't allowed me to "settle down" on earth. He has forced me to "need Heaven." (*N. I.* 162–63)

PRAYER OF SECLUSION

Élise Autissier has taken the first verse of this poem and slipped it into her account of Marie Noël's last days on earth, entitled "Le dernier Noël." *[Auxerre et Marie Noël*, 236] The placing of the verse makes it plain that Autissier herself reads it as a poem written with death in view. Having thought of it originally as one of many poems and passages in the *Notes Intimes* about her need for solitude and silence, I was struck at once that it could be read both ways, and it may well have been Marie Noël's hope that it would. It certainly makes a perfect foil to the poem she chose to close her life's work with, the last poem in this selection, "Where Am I Going...?"

A BIRD

According to Escholier this poem was written at Diges in 1928, but for some reason left in a drawer where it languished, like others, for years before being taken out, tinkered with and finally published. Escholier, who admires it, comments on the eleven-syllable verses: "this awkward rhythm which she handles with such mastery..." (Escholier, 382).

SONG OF THE GIRL OF LITTLE WORTH

A poem dated 1967, it is unlike any other she wrote, and to come up with a one-off in the last months of a long life is as remarkable in its way as the poem. Written in the octosyllables she often uses in her traditional poems and with a repetitive pattern of words and phrases, its setting is not "legendary" but late nineteenth century. It introduces the self-repeating story of the girl seduced and abandoned by her lover to die in destitution, leaving a motherless child to recommence the cycle. Among many variants, Marie Noël could well have heard at twenty a French music-hall song which retained its popularity for more than fifty years and may still survive on YouTube... She will also, during her years of parish work, have met with examples of the real-life equivalent. Her genius lies in taking a tragedy that has been sentimentalised, and lifting it to an Alpine height. Moreover, in doing so, she manages to spell prostitution with the eight letters that make up *deux sous*.

CHILD'S SONG

> This tale the wise have never heard
> I wrote it out of season
> For those too young to have acquired
> And those who've lost their reason. (*Chants des Quatre-Temps*, 16)

The last of many, mostly sung by nurses. Marie Noël's poems and prose are full of children—listening, laughing, weeping, dying, babies at the breast, a child coming home in tears from school—all the children she never had, running beside her down the road.

THE DESERTER

The Lover has a Beloved, who is all things good, described in lines of particular beauty. This is surely the soul in her baptismal robe. He reveres her, but only in church on Sundays. Summer's heat brings pestilence: the basilisk comes slithering up, encircling the lover with lies. He continues fawning on the Beloved while polluting all around her, until suddenly with an open, guileless face, he tramples in the mud her spotless robe and walks away. Marie Noël has written plenty of poems about faithless lovers, but this one, with the contrast between the verses given to the beloved, and the creeping menace of the basilisk which in the end becomes one with the lover, has a particular power.

Footpaths through the last years

> Extreme old age strikes me as being an age of poetry, alike in that to early childhood. In these twilight years at either end of life, the hard light of day has not yet dissipated, or never more will, the shadows of eternity which book-end our bright years.
>
> Just as a child will use an expression that seems to gush out from some pre-natal fount, there are cries of the old which rise from unknown wells that reason has no access to.
>
> Of these poor people whose light has dimmed, we say "they have lost their minds."
>
> That is true, what they now have are those eyes of the soul which look back, through the dark, to an eternal seeing. (*N. I.* 275)

Marie Noël gave death as one of the three main themes of her poetry, and wrote of it also at length in her Journal, though rarely, if at all, after 1940. It is thus to these last poems that we must turn to learn how she met these final years and whether she was at last freed from the dread she had harboured since childhood in her heart.

WHEN THE DOG ROSE OF SUMMER

> Walking to her dying day
> God knows her but did not say,
> Never grand among the great
> With the smallest smaller yet. (*Chants des Quatre-Temps*, 101)

APRIL'S DAY

> Poetry contains no positive reality.
>
> There is in it a deep life, an intense and transfiguring emotion, on which the circumstances arousing these have little bearing. When the chosen moment comes, some next to nothing may suffice to spark off the inspiration which, seizing hold of it, amplifies it without limits.
>
> Dante catches sight of Beatrice. Beatrice? Has he known her long, paid court to her? Maybe...maybe not. Every eventuality in the song lies hidden in the poet.
>
> And if, what is more, this poet is an artist, it can happen that a number of impressions may fuse in the poet's mind into one. There are sculptors who have drawn their gods from several models.
>
> The charm of a poem is often gravely impaired, even demolished, by attempts to situate, date it and box it in on all sides like some poor scrap of human identity. Poetry, like religion needs mystery.
>
> The proper place for the Host is in the tabernacle not on the shelves of the kitchen dresser.

These thoughts on poetry (reproduced without date or source as "inédits" in Gallimard's 2003 edition of *Chants de la Merci et Chants des Quatre Temps*) could have been written for this poem which exists in a heaven of its own.

It offers a narrative of sorts, tied to reality by the thinnest of silken threads: once upon a time there was a Day which left happy memories; these memories have been revisited by the poet, laid to rest and blessed; we too are blest to be allowed into this woodland grove, where all is now at peace; there is nothing on the kitchen dresser except a few plates.

Marie Noël, perhaps unfortunately, continues: "Learn to read the poets. Don't read them like 'journalists.'" This is an embarrassing challenge, as I am about to do just this, in the case of this poem and four others, all contained in this Ember Day collection, all linked by internal references, as also by dates both printed underneath and scattered through the poems. These poems, I will suggest, hide a narrative, which a part of her is under irresistible pressure to bring to life in written form. She doesn't do it for us, but for herself, to ensure that it still lives, and grows, and changes. I am also pretty sure that she enjoyed playing this variation on hide-and-seek: Abbé Bremond's "espièglerie angélique" popped up in many forms.

The first poem of the quintet is dressed in medieval costume: a knight rides into town in search of a song: first he meets with a cold rain-shower, then a bolted door. Behind it a pious woman is saying her rosary. They engage in conversation. He asks her for a song, she has three, two for the Virgin, the third and most beautiful she finds several excuses for not giving him: she has planted it in her garden, it hasn't yet grown, she is waiting for a rain-shower, for the sky to fall into her heart. At this point the knight gets the message and rides away. This poem is entitled "Chanson d'Avril" and carries below the date April 18th, 1967. It is followed at intervals by four more poems, the first, "Bien Peu..." bears the date April 18th, 1965, and laments how little is left of the original day now lost in passing time; the knight has turned into a weary old man, the song writer into an old maid who can no longer see where she is going. The words *éteule*, stubble and *crapaud*, toad, and notably the second, are echoes of two poems in the *Automne* collection [*Plainte dans le Soir* and *Chant du Crapaud*]. Finally, the current April Day on which she is again writing comes to weep over April gone: "so little" is left, nothing perhaps, but wait—*love that has no age and is not tied to time lives on ...*

The next two poems in the book, "April's Day" [*Jour*] and *Fidélité* are dated 1966 and 1964, and establish themselves also as anniversary poems. The first adds the detail that the original Day was Easter Tuesday, and both are again related by internal cross-referencing to the two just discussed as well as to earlier poems. In *Fidélité* the old man reappears, compared now to a long river whose many loves have been poured out into the sea, but one was different—a tiny streamlet running down from Alpine snows in spring, and God will preserve in him this stream in its fierce purity, returning it at the last, along with his own troubled waters, to the divine source.

"Alleluia," last of the five poems, brings closure. They make a remarkable little group, tightly interrelated, reflective, tender, and telling a story of a love which persisted in despite—or perhaps because—of a refusal: the refusal of a woman rejected at least once and broken by the experience. She manages refusal with an admirable grace that even the Knight appears to have accepted. Why did she turn him down? Maybe she had no wish to be another on his list; maybe she found herself free for the first time in her life to pray, to write, to organise her days; maybe it was too late for that particular commitment. But Blessed Saint Tuesday, which in 1967 did in fact fall on April 18th, would never be forgotten, it would always be the Day of Days.

(Regarding the importance of particular days, there is also an echo of three verses from a chapter of Ecclesiasticus [33:7, 10, 12], which we know she read because she cites another passage from it in her Journal [*N. I.* 315]. I quote from the Douai Bible, because it is translated from the Vulgate, as will have been French Bibles in use before Vatican II. "Some of them God made high and great days, and some of them he put in the number of ordinary days. Some of them hath he blessed, and exalted: and some of them hath he sanctified, and set near Himself" [Ecclus. 33:10 and 12].)

ALLELUIA

The last of these poems bearing in full the fated date. Did she really, aged eighty-two, write three significant poems on that day? Surely not. Around that time, perhaps. Are these dates saying: Look at me! Look at me, and read me if you can! Not quite. I think she thought she was too clever for her readers and thereby safe. She was telling her truth to herself, bringing it to life, celebrating it as infinitely precious, not only in this life, but in eternity. And since that truth was not intended to be shared with us, the poems should be read with that in mind, and with care to leave room for the spiritual dimension that is intrinsic to her poetry.

"Alleluia" is the shortest of the five. All has been said, but poets can ring changes with the same bells. In its last line she boldly confounds the Psalmist [Ps. 30 (29):9]: our very dust will praise our God, Alleluia!

SWAN SONG

This poem was important to her. She gives it the title *Soir*, adding *Chant du cygne* in smaller print: swans sing only once. It is dated 1963, her eightieth year, and like her other late poems it is not easy. The syntax in particular is very dense and the meaning has to be teased out, it is like unpicking embroidery.

The first verse signals the summing up of a life, and already there is a drum beat: the words "She is there" figure six times in the poem: she is there at the beginning of each verse, there too at the end of life's road, looking back, waiting...

The core of the poem is about forgiveness, the resolution of past and present. The wound in her heart is still there, open, and she wouldn't have it any other way; it is her most precious possession—her *déchirure*—the only thing she has to offer. She looks back at the past: it also is wounded, and to some degree still unhealed; it must not be allowed to become scarred over with resentment. Having recalled the hurts done to her, washed and wiped the feet of those passing before her, she sees an area ahead still unexplored. What or Who is this Evil [*le Mal*] that appears in the last three lines? Is it one, or two, entities or persons? It appears to be layered in meaning, as her own perception has become with age. As she looks back, she sees in it the ill-will lying at the root of all sin and hurt: what's done is done, but, forgiven, it can no longer harm. Looking forward, it is Evil looming as Death, the last enemy [1 Cor. 15:26], but which has lost its terror for her who no longer resists it, for, with this acceptance, love will cast out fear.

There is a mysterious allusion to Satan disguising himself as an angel of light [2 Cor. 11:14], to which the key lies in the poem "Evening Hymn" [p. 132] where death is both a horrifying prospect and a devilish invention: the poet nonetheless hopes that when it has done its worst, death may turn on her a resplendent face. The first and principal meaning of *splendide* in French, as of *splendidus* in Latin is "dazzling, glorious." I am not aware of Marie Noël using it elsewhere, and it turns this late and outwardly sombre poem into a celebration of her freeing from a fear which has haunted her since early childhood. Death has become the door to glory.

THE GREYHOUND

> The ultimate distress: that of animals.
>
> That of the old dog that hears its death approaching and runs off...
>
> ...Mankind manages to transfigure death to some degree using the perspective of religion.
>
> But in animals the distress is irremediable, present in the eyes of the creature that knows its sentence. (*N. I.* 129)

This poem, like "Swan Song" as difficult as it is rewarding, may well have been her last; it is dated 1967. It is arcane, because she is straining to see into the unknowable and to say the unsayable. During her last few years she wrote increasingly in a vernacular refined by time, that only she by then fully understood. Familiarity is the only lexicon, and I suggest following her again down the paths signposted by "key-words," in particular those for *tenderness,* and not forgetting *déchiré*, torn, rent.

That the presence of the greyhound is central is made clear in her Introduction by its connection with the supreme moment in the narrative of Christ's Passion, the "animal cry." The faithful hound is the animal in us, the flesh that plays the principal role in our dying. He is the first to hear the call, the one to lead the way. He is a royal dog (one of those which end up sculpted on tombs), and his Queen hurries after him. She has plenty to think about, and so do we. A change of dress, for a start. Not the one that fame has given her, but the most torn one, *la robe la plus déchirée*, the one first met with in "The Face," and then again in "The Song of the Robe," the robe of suffering [see above, 98/219 and 152/235].

Returning to "The Greyhound" with these images in mind ... the Queen wears her torn dress, sweating, at a feast where she is required to drain her chalice; her friends meanwhile sleep in the garden. There are obvious clues to unpick here: Gethsemane... perhaps Bellevue, which was her Passiontide ...Wounds are now her only ornaments. As in the "Song of the Robe," it is the flesh that is torn at the last. Roses, much loved in life, are now redundant, dismissed in the almost identical words attributed to Bossuet thirty years earlier [*N. I.* 160, and above, 207], and which have now become apt.

She moves through and beyond time and space. All that is left is the greyhound just ahead, and she encourages him to go on without her (maybe a reference to a possible loss of consciousness?), and to give, should he meet him, a silent message to one who made of her briefly a queen in the land of exile. A rival king? Long ago, perhaps, for a time, as representing here the love that should have blossomed into a home and children: desire like a tear, a *déchirure*, in the heart. The greyhound is to lick his hand in passing, as briefly as she was his queen—this is the final forgiveness, the one that has cost her the most, the wound that never ceased bleeding.

A powerful poem, unique to her and in the context of her work: there seems to be no limit to the range of her imagination.

WHERE AM I GOING? ...

The poem with which she chose to close her life's work was written in 1966, three years after "Swan Song," a year before "The Greyhound." Composed in memory of Daniel-Rops, a writer she knew and admired who had died some months earlier [*Auxerre et M. N.*, 58], it represents a tribute to a member of the Académie, and plainly reflects her life, not his.

She has come a long way from "Closure" and "Old Woman." All sense of failure has gone. Here is the boat waiting at the quayside to carry her out to sea. We are somewhere strangely impersonal, with someone we no longer quite know. In the first three verses she is half with us, measuring her past life in terms of time and space. In the third verse she slips anchor and is gone with God, a God we do not quite know either, as she has never presented him like this. Perhaps we need to go back a little to see what has been happening.

In the last dated entry in the *Notes Intimes* Marie Noël brings back unexpectedly the inscrutable God of the 1920s, the one of whom she said: "Mon Dieu, je ne vous aime pas." Now we are in 1958 and he is telling his creature that she will soon be broken and replaced: "But that, little girl of no worth, who will have served me willy-nilly, that will be for you the beginning of everlasting mercy." It is one of those moments when one is not surprised she didn't like him much.

From then on there are only poems, and the snippets of prose gathered after her death. Nor does God reappear in that particular guise: all indications point to her last years being a time of healing for heart and for head. But grace, as ever, had a part to play. In the summer of 1957, her eyes had lit on these verses of Ecclesiasticus—"as dazzling as lightning," she calls them:

> Consider all the works of the Lord,
> you will find they go in pairs, by opposites.
> Opposite evil stands good,
> opposite death, life;
> so too opposite the devout stands the sinner. [33:14, 15; also quoted 42:24, 25]

Her thoughts run on for a while on this track:

> Good and evil are not, as I so long thought, irreconcilable adversaries...two parallel powers which will never come together.
>
> There is between them merely a distance—for us unmeasurable, there is between them just a time-lag of inconceivable limits. (*N. I.* 315, 317)

The recognition and resolution of paradox. It had indeed taken a long time. In "Where Am I Going?" she is on the verge of that "eternal" seeing where opposites come together—*finita jam sunt proelia.*

Halfway through the poem, the words of time and place which have anchored and measured her life make space for God, where it appears in the last two lines of verse 3 that the incarnate Son is de-fathering the Father. The fatherhood of God has long been for Marie Noël a dubious symbol, and not without reason [*N. I.* 101]; the subconscious threat of male power surely lies at the bottom of the abyss. Here she recognises fully that Christ has taken her in all security from that, now unnecessary symbol, to Love itself, unportrayed and unportrayable. Three months before composing this poem she wrote the following:

> Our path
> From God-Love to God-Love, through Christ-Love. [*Auxerre et M. N.*, 21]

From the Beginning to the End, through the Word. The poet is now "lost," "out at sea," there is "nothing," "not even an island." Space is a blur. Time is no more. God, whose face has at times petrified her, is faceless, he has become the translucence that is Love. The final line consists of two syllables: "m'attend," "awaits me." Are we back in time? No, for love is not measured in time, but in intensity of yearning: she has taken us with her into in a new dimension.

BIBLIOGRAPHY

POETRY

Les Chansons et Les Heures (1920).

Les Chants de la Merci (1930).

Le Rosaire des joies (1930).

Chants et psaumes d'automne (1947).

Chants d'arrière-saison (Stock, 1961).

Œuvre poétique (Stock, 1956). Contains the first four titles listed above; new edition (posthumous), 1971, adds *Chants d'arrière-saison* .

Chants des Quatre-Temps (Stock, 1972).

PROSE WORKS

Contes—including *Le Chemin d'Anna Bargeton* (1944); reprinted without *Le Chemin d'Anna Bargeton* (1949).

Notes intimes (Stock, 1959).

Petit-jour (Stock, 1951); reprinted as *Petit-jour et Souvenirs du beau mai* (1964).

Le Cru d'Auxerre (1967).

La Rose rouge (1957); with *L'Âme en peine* (1954) *et autres contes* (Stock, 1960).

Auxerre et Marie Noël, ed. Elise Autissier (Zodiaque, 1992). Contains unpublished material from her late years, as well as the *Chants des Quatre-Temps*, and the account of her last day through to the small hours.

Almanach pour une jeune fille triste (Desclée de Brouwer, 2011). A collection of *pensées* varying from one line to a page drawn from many sources, some from her own pen, and dating from the Bellevue period. The manuscript was found after her death and published in 2011 with the author's preface and an introduction by Chrystelle Claude.

J'ai bien souvent de la peine avec Dieu : Correspondance Marie Noël-Abbé Mugnier, ed. Xavier Galmiche (Cerf, 2017).

SECONDARY WORKS

Since this book is not primarily intended for an academic audience, I mention only two titles that I have found particularly useful.

Escholier, Raymond, *La Neige qui brûle* (Fayard, 1957). Indispensable.

Lobet, Benoît, *Mon Dieu, je ne vous aime pas. Foi et spiritualité chez Marie Noël* (Stock, 1994). Written by a perceptive theologian.

CLUNY MEDIA

Designed by Fiona Cecile Clarke, the Cluny Media *logo depicts a monk at work in the scriptorium, with a cat sitting at his feet.*

The monk represents our mission to emulate the invaluable contributions of the monks of Cluny in preserving the libraries of the West, our strivings to know and love the truth.

The cat at the monk's feet is Pangur Bán, from the eponymous Irish poem of the 9th century. The anonymous poet compares his scholarly pursuit of truth with the cat's happy hunting of mice. The depiction of Pangur Bán is an homage to the work of the monks of Irish monasteries and a sign of the joy we at Cluny take in our trade.

"Messe ocus Pangur Bán,
cechtar nathar fria saindan:
bíth a menmasam fri seilgg,
mu memna céin im saincheirdd."

Printed in Great Britain
by Amazon

60559664R00161